# How To Be
## A Better
# PERSON

Dr. Gilbert Edwards

authorHOUSE®

AuthorHouse™
1663 Liberty Drive
Bloomington, IN 47403
www.authorhouse.com
Phone: 1 (800) 839-8640

Published by AuthorHouse 03/21/2017

ISBN: 978-1-5246-8520-1 (sc)
ISBN: 978-1-5246-8519-5 (e)

Dedicated To

My Loving Wife

Dorothy M. Edwards

Who has been my wife for over fifty years!

# PREFACE

Through the years, I have noticed that many people have lost many things such as; marriage, break-up of friendships, etc. I feel that it is because of bad character. I feel a need to reach out to those who need to build a better character; to make themselves better.

There is a need for one to behave oneself in a manner to be an example to their family, or to those that are around them. One should take time to be a better person. Therefore, one should try and study hard to build their character. In my study, I feel that an early age should begin to build a good character. There should be a place for developing Christian character. Sunday school seems to be the place. Sunday-school teaching is spiritual work. It means soul culture. When the Sunday school pupil has been won to Christ, the work has been, but fairly begun.

Everything must now be done to help the pupil to form habits of Christian living. The prayer life must be strengthened; Bible Study must be encouraged; and the graces of the spirit must be acquired. Self-mastery must be won.

# TABLE OF CONTENTS

# INTRODUCTION

The author is writing to encourage those who may read this book to be a better person by improving their character. The author will try to explain how to build a good character through education such as; the process of receiving systematic instructions; a body of knowledge. True wisdom promotes health, well-being and happiness. Many of the problems that plaque human existence springs from poor judgment, foolish choices and confused values.

There must be instructions to learn from. Instructions refer to a process of training in which the learner submits to the teaching and guidance of a wise person. In order to benefit from such instruction, one must cultivate a teachable spirit and accept the discipline of firm guidance. The ultimate reward of instruction and training (conduct, behavior, ethics and character) will be a long and useful life.

Moral instruction prevents the heart from swaying to and fro with the winds of physical desire and passion. Instead, it keeps the heart fixed on the path of wisdom. If no one is willing to teach you for free, then hire a teacher; for you cannot arrive at wisdom instantly. It is your life; a human is only given life so that he can overcome his negative traits. A person must always improve; for if he does not, what is his justification for living?

The development of the mind must start at an early age. This is done by educating the mind of a child. The word "education" comes from a word meaning "to lead out"; to lead the child out to meet the experiences of life; to lead the child to feel, to think and do right, to himself, to his fellow men and his God. But, someone needs to teach him. There are two types of children with two different characters, motor and sensory.

The Motor Child, impulsive and enthusiastic; he is quick to comprehend and to decide, but is as quick to change his mind. Action precedes deliberation. He requires knowledge readily and forgets even more easily.

The Sensory Child, is quiet and thoughtful, slower to respond, but steadier when turned. He is possibly less attractive at first, but he wears well. It is more difficult for him to acquire knowledge, but he retains for a long time what he has learned.

There must be a mental development. The mental life is developed through the use of the senses. There is also a moral development. Justice, unselfish and loyalty are virtues The child conscience awakens, the moral sense is not as strong as it will be later, but at this age the child has an increasing sense of the difference between right and wrong, and should be encouraged to form habits of formal living. Spiritual development, the child in the home, and loving God from his earliest recollection should grow naturally into Christian experiences.

## Character

Character is destiny. It will get you where you want to go. In every one of us there are two ruling and directing principles; whose guidance we follow wherever they may lead; the one being an innate desire of pleasure; the other, an acquired judgement which aspires after excellence – Socrates as quoted in Plato's Phaedrus.

There are more important lessons to learn or habits to be formed than that of right judgment and of delighting in good character and noble actions. – Aristotle, Politics.

# CHAPTER I

# THE PURPOSE OF BEING
# A BETTER PERSON

B etter than bad – a more excellent or effective type or quality person; a better father for the family, a better leader or employee, or maybe a better friend. A good father will take care or be concerned about the responsibilities of his family. Christian leaders, social leaders- those who are chosen to watch over the spiritual or social welfare of a local church, or work place must possess the highest personal and moral qualities. First as representatives of the church or a work place, or even as a leader in the home; and to the community as an example to church members, workers at the work place and at home.

They must be above reproach in their life-styles, they must be given to pride or greed, and must be faithful in marriage. Be a better person to make someone happy. Be better than you used to be. Be better so you can make someone else better.

There is a purpose in God's creation for all of us. The world that God created is constituted in such a way that those who cooperate with God's basic laws find the natural world sustains their life. God's natural and moral laws makes sense when viewed from the Creator's wisdom. To obey these laws shows good judgment, so there is a law of being good. Live so that someone will want to be with you. No one wants to be with or around a bad person. It is not all the time that people want your money; it is you they want. We spend more time trying to get money and seem to forget about the one who loves us. Wealth is not the final good; it carries potentially devastating power for character. It cannot satisfy the claim for right relationship. Wealth cannot purchase respect and good relationships in this life. Neither can it provide safety from God's judgment. Even in this life, a good salary does not purchase life's truly basic needs.

Two groups of people comprise every society; the righteous and the wicked. The righteous are in right standing with God (the one who wrote the laws of love), standing in God's way of life, experiencing God's deliverance and society's admiration. The wicked opposes God and His ways depending rather on human guile, desires and wealth.

Be better to place a high priority on the family. The father must be a provider of care for his family. Meeting the physical needs of the family is a part of the father's stewardship. Fathers should manage personal resources in a responsible way to care for the family needs. To fail to fulfill family responsibilities is a sin.

Spiritual leaders, those who are chosen to watch over the spiritual welfare of a local church, must possess the highest personal and moral qualities. Therefore, they improve to be better. As representatives of the church to the community, and as examples to members, they must not be given to pride or greed, and must be faithful in marriage. Since they are responsible for teaching and preaching, they should possess the gifts necessary for fulfilling these functions. They must be well trained and well-grounded in the faith to be able to impart sound doctrine and to guard the church from error. Since they are charged with exercising oversight, they should show evidence of a gift for personal relationships. They should not be violent or quarrelsome, overbearing or quick tempered. As leaders of the Church family, they should model a well-ordered family life in their own homes. They must also be hospitable to receive travelling Christians, as well as the poor, as guest. Leaders must set examples for others to follow. Getting drunk is not excusable for a leader. A person is to be better to assure their role in marriage, as a family.

Home relationships should honor the Lordship of Christ over the home and demonstrate to the outside world the power of the Word of God. The love shown in a Christian home should overcome non-Christian's arguments against Christianity. In family relation, each person, that is the husband and wife, should respect each other's role in the household duties. In Titus, stronger emphasis is given to the importance of personal self-control and self-giving in order that outsiders may not be able to criticize the behavior of Christians. Men are to exemplify self-control; older women are to demonstrate reverent submission to Christ; and younger women are to honor their husbands through yielding in love to their headship in the home. (Titus 2:2-10) To be better, the family will have to stick together.

Paul applied the concept of mutual submission to Christian family relationships; husband-wife, parent-child. In each case, self-giving of one to the other is described. For the wife, it is voluntarily yielding in love to her husband's headship in the home. The husband is to yield himself to his wife in the same spirit that Christ yielded Himself to the cross to establish the Church. Children are to submit themselves to their parent in obedience, and fathers are to give themselves to the task of guidance and discipline for their children (Colossians 3:18-21). One of the purposes for being better is so that your wife will not hinder your prayer. The prayer of a husband and wife is important and must not be hindered by misunderstandings in the relationship. The physical strength of men should not become an obstacle to the joint humility required in any praying together (I Peter 3:7). You will have to get better in order to be good. The good man brings good things out. Just as a good tree bears good fruit (Matthew 7:17).

Be better to make someone else better. Our words indicate our goals. If we want to bring peace and good to the world, we must not speak evil or lie about other people. We must proceed from rejecting evil to choosing and acting upon virtues which are positive. What and how we say things is an indicator of our true spirit. Our religious talk is only as good as our ethical action. God's judgment is lodged against speech, which does not exemplify the love of for your neighbor. God's judgments rest on those who publicly profess religious faith in rituals and ceremonies, but they do not do what they have committed themselves to, while forgetting God destroys human life.

Doing wrong cannot make you good. Sin is wrong doing. Sin needs not to control a person's life. The proper function of guilt is to lead us to take full responsibility for our sin, to recognize that sin ultimately relates to God and alienates us from Him, and to confess God's justice rather than trying to justify ourselves. People are born with a nature prone to sin inherited from their parents (Adam and Eve). Yes, this line goes all the way back to Adam and Eve, but we don't have to stay that way. We can be better. Be good so that someone can love you. Friendship born of common, shared experiences is a most precious possession. When such a relationship is broken and betrayed, the resulting experience is utterly overwhelming. Love, shared in friendship always carries the risk of betrayal.

# Chapter II

# Building A Good Character

Love and faithfulness are two keys biblical virtues. They are the focal point for the understanding and implementation of other virtues such as peace, mercy, justice and righteousness. Love is a self-denying readiness to help other people. It represents a reciprocal relationship of service beyond social duties. Faithfulness indicates trustworthiness, reliability and loyalty. These characteristics can be found in people who please God.

One with integrity of purpose and character will live a life of openness before God and others. Those without such integrity must constantly work at keeping up a front wondering when they will be caught in their own trap of lies. The work of love is to bring smoothness to relationships. Such love does not gloss over difficult; rather, it provides the energy needed to bring the sometimes difficult results of forgiveness and reconciliation. Dishonesty is the opposite of the character traits God calls for and honors; justice, mercy, lovingkindness and righteousness. Persons of integrity are marked by patience, slowness to anger and humility. They are teachable.

Character traits affect our physical health, as well as our relationships with God and man. Quick temper, envy and oppression are foolish traits to cultivate. Patience is the opposite of quick temper. Peaceful hearts do not envy others, and kindness leaves no room for envy. Financial prosperity and social acceptance do not indicate a person is successful in life, or right with God. Contentment and strong personal relationships are more important. A right understanding of love will usher in forgiveness and forgetfulness about an offensive act. Character is shown by our ability to form friendships. Friends never desert or ignore you; work for good and justice. The results will allow others more possibilities for doing the work of justice. Wicked advisers can destroy a ruler.

The goal of society should be establishing right and justice because God loves and embodies these characteristics. The promise of God's protection, blessing and joy resides with those who "love the Lord." To love Him is more than emotion. It is a commitment to hate evil, and therefore, avoid evil actions. God is the believer's ultimate judge of character, advocate of character and resource for activating righteous character. The person seeking growth in Christian grace and character should therefore begin and continue in the ethical light and warmth of God Himself. God's character and ways on behalf of the down and out are well-known. Those who are God's people will surely act as He does. People who do not act like God reveals some of their true character. Good company builds good character.

Participation in evil practices with evil people destroys character. Jesus addressed a problem of major proportions in relationships that of noticing others' personality flaws to the exclusion of our own weakness. The approach of true humility recognizes and begins work on our own faults first. We will do this when we step in the other person's shoes and judge things from that perspective (Matthew 7:1-5, 12). To understand Jesus' instructions about humility, you must observe children. Their sense of innocence, directness and trust gives us keys to comprehending what is means to be humble in the Kingdom of God, This humility is acted out before God, but its credibility is visible as we act toward others with a true sense of their worth and of the gifts they bring to the Kingdom's work. (Matthew 18:1-10)

One of the greatest barriers to Christian maturity is knowing what to do with forgiveness. Jesus' use of exaggeration makes the point that one forgives and forgives; there is no limit. How long does it take until you have worked through forgiveness? Until you can want the well-being of the other who has trespassed against you. The importance of Jesus' teaching here is that our lack of willingness to forgive our neighbor acts as a barrier to accepting God's forgiveness of our own sin (Matthew 18:21-25). Personal character grows out of love for God. Loving God leads us to love other people. Evil character causes people to reject Jesus Christ, people are totally devoted in love to the darkness of the world's way, or they are ready to have their lives examined and changed by the light of the world, Jesus. Persons devoted to evil fear what light would reveal in their lives.

Persons dedicated to truth in knowledge and in action come to Jesus Christ and give evidence that God is at work in Jesus Christ's coming. Build good character by having a prayer life. Peter was a man of prayer (Peter 3:1; 9:40). Grace that saved us is not a license to sin or live in any manner we please. The grace that frees us from sin is also the resource to live a life of obedient love to the call of God. To do the will of God involves a disciplined application of our will in the matter of life. This begins with a goal to do good rather than evil to other persons no matter how they treat us. It rests on an attitude of love and respect for others. It involves personal humility. Good character builds a reputation. Integrity of character involves respect for our physical bodies. Our bodies are to represent Jesus Christ and do nothing which would bring shame on His name. Character reveals itself in humble concern for other people rather than in proud display of superior knowledge Theological understanding may give us freedom, but Christian character will lead us to limit freedom out of love for a person with differing theological understanding, Christians are strong, courageous and persistent; they are not abrasive and hardheaded. Standing firm should be in loving care, not in proud dogmatism. Hold on, persevere, be faithful to the trust put in you and have courage.

The application of doing good is broad. We should do good to those like us, but also to those different from us. The motivation for doing good is many fold because: God expects it of us; human creatures made in the image of God need good and not bad; and doing good provides a basis for further witness of the gospel's redemptive power. The Christian should present a life-style to the world which projects a stunk contrast to the world's ways. A life that exhibits thanksgiving and peace is desired. Christian character shows itself in making the best decisions for all concerned. Imitation of Jesus Christ's life of humility in interpersonal relationships will produce a life of purity with one another; choose and cultivate this approach. Study Jesus' life through the gospels. Paul's relationship with Christ provided him joy. He called Christians to the same sense of rejoicing. Rather than dwelling on the past, which cannot be changed, Paul exhorted Christians to keep their eyes on the forward pull of Jesus Christ (Philippians 3:1-11). Rejoice in God; be full of thanksgiving toward Him. Such attitudes bring the sense of fulfillment and joy in God that affects all of our relationships. This is God's peace; a peace so wonderful the human mind cannot fully understand it. This peace can be a present reality for the person who gently and kindly lives life by letting God take care of anxieties.

Prayer is the lifeline to peace. To identify what is the will of God, Christians need consciously to think on the positive dimensions of life and being confident of his own standing with Jesus Christ. Paul contrasted the development of character as proposed by the pagan world with the Christian approach. Religious rituals and prohibitions do not develop character. Personal character grows, as a part of the Church (Christ's body). Only as we are directly connected with Jesus Christ do we grow. Such growth leads us away from self-indulgence of worldly desires to be like Christ (Colossians 2:13-23).

On pattern of ethical living is to put off the negative and put on the positive. Positive Christian attitudes turn attention away from personal desires and achievements to relations with and needs of others. Love is the center from which all other Christian attitudes flow. Paul appealed to two motivations for the Thessalonians to live up to high ethical standards. One was to please God. The other was to live so as to win the respect of those outside the gospel. If persons knew only these two guidelines, they would be enough to begin and continue the journey of growing toward mature Christian character. The Christian call is always to improve on what we are already doing (I Thessalonian 4:1-12). Self-control is a primary ingredient of Christian character. A Christian has responsibility to choose to will to do the right and reject the wrong.

The life of peace characterized by a spirit of forgiveness and reconciliation is to be a distinguishing facet of the Christian's life-style. This peace can be recognized by its application to prevent boiling over of quarrels into full scale breakdowns in relationships and by its continual presence in all day to day activity. Losing control affects our whole being. Gaining the control of your anger can provide a key to the maturing expression of more positive virtue in your character. Social harmony, humility, empathy and love are components of Christian character. Christian character centers on knowing and doing the will of God, not on giving in to fleshly lusts or worldly pressures to conform. Respect for others, humility, freedom from anxiety and self-control are Christian character traits. Eschatology, or the doctrine of last things, encourage us to develop a holy character like God's.

The twists and turns of life ought not to be perceived by the Christian as the acts of a capricious God. Rather, they are challenges to our attention skills, testing if we are seeking the will of God. Following God's commands develops our character. Mourning and lamenting are proper ways to seek God's will in times of danger and/or loss. God's commands from the basis for settling human disputes. Every society must have a just system for settling disputes, or everyone will feel free to ignore moral limits placed on us by the rights of others. Teaching and demonstration are part of God's mechanism to have character expectations placed before us. We are obligated to learn God's moral expectations and obey them. The core attitude for stealing is covetousness. God intends that the inner character damage done by coveting is severe. The society God intends for His people is based on love for the neighbor, not envy.

Acts of obeying God in and out of themselves serve to reflect our true character. Inherent in God's moral imperative is the expectancy of human response. This expectancy is based on the human creature's characteristic of being a choice maker. We can reject or adopt the imperative that reflects our true character. Obedience to God is not halfhearted, but requires investment of one's self. Following God's guidelines for character includes acting with resolve and courage. Courage as a biblical virtue has parallels in perseverance, consistency and forth-rightness.

God's inspired word is the source for building godly character. Personal character is not a secret. Those we associate with daily know our character. We need to hear their testimony and be ready to make necessary changes. Integrity of personal character finds its roots in a relationship with God. Job's confession of integrity ranks with the expectation of character given in Isaiah 1:11-17. Job invited specific cures on his life from God, if he had committed the sins surveyed. His statement covers virtually every aspect of personality and life; the sexual dimension; the sphere of economics; treatment of the needy; attitude toward enemies; and responsibility as a steward of creation. The implicit understanding is that his relationship with God shaped his character, as well as provided the grounding and energy for living life on such an ethical plane.

God's people are marked by consciousness of God which pervades all of life. God's ways are a source of guidance, encouragement and moral strength for us. God's people portray patterns of integrity to their society and are known for their moral uprightness based on obedience to God's word. Other people display opposite characteristics. They are wicked and face condemnation. Arrogance has no place in the believer's character. All that we are comes by God's grace. Therefore, those preen and posture before others will suffer God's judgment because of their lack of humility.

Building our lives around the moral expectations of God will produce a shield of encouragement against the insults of those alienated from God. Contriteness or sadness over one's spiritual state is a mark of one who seeks God's face. Such contriteness will be honored by God's comforting presence. One cannot compartmentalize worship into one phase of life while carrying on a life-style of overt hypocrisy and detestable actions. All of life is under God's judgment and should be offered to God. Integrity of character can be marked by one's sense of purpose in life. Is this purpose of a single strand, that is, seeking the will of God; or, does it reflect a fragmentation going off in many directions? Singleness of heart and action after God's purposes reveal one in whom God is working His grace. Daniel's trustworthy character gained him the reputation of being obedient to his God no matter what. Ethical behavior is rooted in strong personal devotion (Daniel 6:4-5).

Pride in human ingenuity and security is blind to the matter of God's all seeing-eye. Such pride is antithetical to the person of God. Micah related the hopelessness of the human condition around him. Despair, frustration and futility typified the reactions of some, but Micah hoped in God's sovereign justice. Such hope is a shaper of character and conduct (Micah 7:1-7).

Paul speaks of man's character in the last days:

"This know also, that in the last days perilous times shall come. For men shall be lovers of their own selves, covetous, boasters, proud, blasphemers, disobedient to parents, unthankful, unholy, without natural affection, trucebreakers, false accusers, incontinent, fierce, despisers of those that are good, traitors, heady, high-minded, lovers of pleasures more than lovers of God; having a form of godliness but denying the power thereof; from such turn away. For of this sort are they which creep into houses, and lead captive silly women laden with sins, lead away with divers lusts, ever learning, and never able to come to the knowledge of the truth . . . men of corrupt minds, reprobates concerning the faith." (II Timothy 3:1-8)

# CHAPTER III

# CHRISTIAN ETHICS

P aul, in the Book of Romans, is exhorting on the basis of Christian conduct, being transformed and making a thorough change in character (Romans 12:12). Paul is inviting them to lead the life of consecration victims. The victim must live to become, at every moment of his existence, the active agent of the divine will. What use is it to be make of this consecrated body? Verse 2 proceeds to answer this question; "And be not conformed to this world; but be ye transformed by the renewing of your mind, that ye may prove what is that good, and acceptable, and perfect will of God."

Don't be conformed to this world; to its sinful spirit, maxims, customs and habits. Don't model after this world, which can be rejected. Love not the world – I John 2:15:

1. To love the world, and the things that are in the world; is to make them our treasure, and put our trust in them, instead of in God.
2. Is not of the Father; does not come from him, and is not on his side, but stands in opposition to him.

He created the world and gave it to men to be used in his service, not to be abused as the minister of fleshly lust.

3. Is of the world; comes from the world as the nourished of earthly lust, and is opposed to God and his service.

What is to be done; seek a new model, superior type to be realized by means of a power acting within? Be transformed by putting yourself under the dominion of a new power which will by an inward necessity transform this use. The renewing of the mind; the faculty by which the soul perceives and discerns the good and the truth. But in our natural state, this faculty is impaired; the reigning love of self-darkens the mind and makes it see things in a purely personal light. The natural mind, mislead, is what Paul calls the carnal mind (under the dominion of the flesh). (Colossians 2:18) This is why the Apostle speaks of the renewing of the mind as a condition of the organic transformation which he requires this faculty, free from the power of the flesh, and replaced under the power of the spirit, must recover the capacity for the discerning of the new model to be realized. The most excellent and subline type, the will of God; to discern exactly the will of God. To prove, to make experience of, for the experience of the excellence of the divine will would not be an affair of the mind only; the whole man would take part in it.

By means of his renewed mind the believer studies and recognizes in every given position the divine will toward him in the circumstances, the duty of the saturation, that his will of God is good. The Apostle explains by the three epithets, (descriptive phrases) with which he qualifies this will; the <u>good</u>, the <u>acceptable</u> and the <u>perfected</u>. Such then, is the normal type to which in all circumstances, we must seek to rise with the mind first, then with the conduct.

Good, in that its directions are free from all connivance (wrong doing) with evil, in any form whatever. Acceptable, the impression produced on men when they contemplate this will realized in the believer's life they cannot help paying it a tribute of admiration, and finding it beautiful as well as good. Perfect, this characteristic follows from the combination of the two preceding. For perfection is goodness united to beauty. Whatever happens, conduct yourself on manners of the gospel of Jesus Christ (Philippians 1:27). Paul also in the Book of Ephesians 4:17-32, contrasted the way of Gentiles and that of the Christians as the difference of darkness and light. He put particular emphasis on the change of attitudes caused by the indwelling of Jesus Christ. Do not let any corrupt talk come out of your mouths, but only what is helpful for building another up. Words that do not strengthen church fellowship should never be uttered. Let your speech be always with grace, seasoned with salt (Colossians 4:6). The two natures in you are contrary, the one to the other, causing you to do the thing that you don't want to do. Walk in the spirit; live under His influence and follow His directions. Do not fulfill the lust of the flesh; don't follow sinful inclination or comply with temptations to sin. Let us walk in the spirit, letting it be conformed to us in character, so that our inward principles, as well as our outward principles, and conduct shall be in harmony with each other.

## Christian Ethics in Relation to Moral Principles

Our ethical freedom carries responsibility. We must consider limitations that God sets on us so we will not infringe upon the freedom of other people or take God's rights to ourselves. The key to the description of Noah (Genesis 6:9, 22) is that he obligated himself to the commands of God. As God's creatures, we live under heavy expectations of conduct. God places imperatives upon us, which it is our duty to perform. As Christians, we will walk through life with God. We also walk with other people, taking society's expectations into account. We must be righteous, living so that the consequences of our actions bear just results for other people both in the short-term and over the long haul of life. Our ethical decisions therefore include theological, societal, relational and consequential aspects. A one sided basis for ethics is not sufficient to meet biblical standards.

The bible speaks about moral insensitivity in Genesis 13:13, the sin of the men of Sodom. Homosexuality was one aspect of their sin, (Genesis 19:4-5) but more was involved. Sin has produced a moral insensitivity on their part. The emphasis here is on the blatant character of their sin. God's people should neither profit nor live with such people, for moral insensitivity is contagious.

Abraham's obedience to God showed two general ethical expectations (Genesis 17:1, 10). General principles for ethical decision making built on a covenant relationship gives direction for specific circumstances. Following God's moral expectations always carries the responsibilities of conveying those expectations to one's family. Our moral development begins through family habits and expectations long before we can learn God's expectations through reading His word. God's expectations are the perfect guidelines of the heavenly Father, leading to righteousness and just. Total allegiance to and trust in God is the foundation for the bible's ethical teachings. Because we know God is good, we do not ask questions here about the morality of God asking Abraham to sacrifice his only son, the son of promise. Rather, we ask if we are trusting enough to obey God's most radical demands on us. Obeying God solidifies each individual's resolve in being a covenant person. Obedience to God also communicates to future generations by action and word of mouth that obedience is the best way to live life. Obedience and celebration are two complementary sides of life in covenant with God. God's imperatives are set out to help us, not to rob us of life's joy. The twists and turns of life ought not to be perceived by the Christian as the acts of a capricious God. Rather, they are challenges to our attention skills, testing if we are seeking the will of God. Following God's commands develops out character. Mourning and lamenting are proper ways to seek God's will in times of danger and/or loss. God's commands form the basis for setting human disputes. Every society must have a just system for settling disputes, or everyone will feel free to ignore moral limits placed on us by the rights of others.

Teaching and demonstration are part of God's mechanism to have character expectations placed before us. We are obligated to learn God's moral expectations and obey them. God's saving actions show His nature and establishes His right to set up moral demands on His people. His demands lead His people to be holy, an example of morality before all other people. God's love for His people is the reason He sets out moral limits for us. Each person is free to make moral choices. Those choices should be made within the responsible boundaries of what God has declared as moral and immoral. Persons and societies outside God's people offer choices which may entice, but such choices are not options if we trust and follow God.

Ungodly society tempts God's people with immoral sexual practices. No human logic can make it right for us to go beyond God's limits in our sexual behavior. Moral limits have enforcement mechanisms in God's relationship with His people. He punishes appropriately those who refuse to trust Him and abide by His limits (Leviticus 18:24-28). Obedience to God's word is possible. God does not set up imperatives we cannot follow. Human weakness is not an acceptable excuse. God calls us to full-time obedience. Reminders of God's moral limits help the child of God remember His expectations and personal promises to obey. Such physical reminders may take various forms. Making and using such reminders should not become laws that people impose on others or use to judge others (Matthew 25:5).

The imperative to hear carries the implicit and explicit note of doing or acting upon what is heard. Listening and learning is not enough. God's people must do what they know and act on what they believe. God's commands to heed and imitate His revealed character gives rise to our reverential worship, from which springs our life style. Our total being should be having a personal character reflecting God's nature. Love for God leads us to accept gladly and obey the moral limits He sets for us. The paradox of following God's moral imperatives is that what looks like it will be so confining is actually liberating to one's spirit. God reminded Israel that they knew what physical slavery was like, if they failed to live by His ethical expectations. They would know of a worse slavery-the slavery of the spirit (Deuteronomy 16:12). Consequences are to be expected when disobedience to God's ethical expectations become a way of life. The cause and effect relationship of obedience and blessing contrasts vividly with the disobedience and judgment pattern in the Old Testament.

Here in Deuteronomy 28:25, the judgment is expressed in terms of military defeat. Therefore, God expressed His displeasure with the Hebrews' disobedience in such a way that they knew there were bounds beyond which their unethical conduct could not go with reprisal. Sin always exacts a price. God's written word reveals His expectations of His people. We are called to follow biblical teachings. Obeying the word in total devotion to God is the essence of biblical ethics. Every person faces ethical choices. The main choice is to serve God or sere something less than God. Choosing to serve God means eliminating certain practices from our lives. God does not give any leader a blank check to follow personal desire. (II Samuel 11:27)

A moral foundation underlies all God's historical acts. Immorality displeases God and brings historical judgment. Refusal to follow God brings lost opportunities. God does not give up. He continues setting His moral imperatives before now generations. God's people need teachers and role models to act as guides for our living together as God's people. God sent His prophets for this purpose. Israel and Judah suffered God's wrath because they chose foreign models instead of God's. We must wisely discern who the proper models are and follow them. The Israelites faced exile because of their determination to step over God's explicit moral boundaries. Their choices for worship and life style values demonstrated poor judgment. Your life style is shaped by whom and what you worship. Life is too important to waste it on idolatrous ways. To identify God's commandments is not enough. The transition of character they can bring begins when you feed upon them and find sustenance for your soul from them. They must become our greatest treasures even in dark days of suffering. The moral law that acts as God's entry level teaches to His ethical expectations of individuals and the larger society.

Stepping over God's moral limits is suicide. Fellowship in community with other people is basic to life. We must exercise care in choosing the community with whom we identify. Friends help form our character. We do not choose friends to reform them. We want them to continue forming our character, leading us to righteousness. The moral guidelines of God to a large extent are obvious, especially to those who desire them. Those who let their relationship to God deteriorate do not easily recognize these guidelines. We are responsible before God to earn what He expects of us. The power of sin to blind us to God's moral guidance is tragically awesome. Eventually, even God will not intervene to stop our rebellion. Moral imperatives are throughout the Bible; this decision making principle appears: look for the good, shun evil (Amos 5:14, 15). When sin so dominates a person that every hour is filled with evil scheming against helpless people, moral values have disappeared. The person has no more moral character.

Humans rebel against moral limits. God responds to continue rebellion by letting people carry their moral freedom of choice to absurd limits. Evil becomes standard operating procedure for such people. Even in the face of death, resulting from their rebellion, they continue devoting themselves to immorality. They lose the ability to distinguish right and wrong, being deaf to God's voice. (Romans 1:28-32) God's moral imperatives are good and holy directing us to life at its best. Our sinful nature rebels at the call to give up any freedom and leads us to do precisely what the law forbids. Law defines good and bad for us. Under sin's leadership we choose the bad. The choice of bad sin deserves death. The choices that face us are sin or Christ. Our model for living and source of will power for living is Jesus Christ. He did all that the law required. He was a perfect, sinless human being. He fulfilled the law's requirements for atonement.

Christian ethics can be briefly summarized; love people and be willing to do for them whatever you would do for yourself. God's imperatives must be consistently applied in al situations. Public opinion should not be the cause of obedience or disobedience. We should not attempt to change back and forth from legalism to grace. We have the responsibility to confront the Church anytime it leads us in any ethical direction which departs from the love of Christ. Certain attitudes and actions are wrong and always will be. Paul proved a long list in II Timothy 3:1-7. The bad life centers on self and sensuality, not on God and others. Evil people manipulate and abuse the needy and weak instead of helping them. Time is too short and important to be wasted in arguments about details. People are too important to be hurt and rejected because they do not agree with us on a matter of interpretation.

## Christian Ethics in Relation to Justice

Injustice surrounds us daily. We must seek God's path toward justice. We only compound the injustice when we attempt to take matters into our own hands. Justice may not always come as soon as we think. It should, but we can be sure that it will come. God will always complete His promises and vindicate His people. Fairness is a primary element of justice; therefore, a certain objectivity must be maintain whether one is poor or rich. Social standing, or lack of it, should not decide whether a person gets fair treatment.

A justice system begins on the local level with neighbors who are just and fair with their neighbors. Justice demands a system of punishment for criminals. Such punishment must not be crueler than the crime. The legal system must protect all people living under its jurisdiction.

Jesus taught that retaliation must not become a law dominating our lives so that we seek reason to punish other persons. Rather we must seek to show God's love to all people. This law of revenge sets guidelines for public justice, not demands for private relationships. It leads society to bring the least harm to the most innocent of society. Society must carefully observe individual rights. Individuals should have the freedom to press for what they justly deserve within society. We cannot categorize people by race, color, bank account, sex or cultural background; and therefore, eliminate some from sharing legal rights.

Justice involves protection for the accused until their cases can be fairly judged. A system of justice depends on proper use of evidence and ethical judges. More than one witness is needed to provide convicting evidence. Intention plays a strong role in biblical ethics. Justice is decided on a person's attitudes and purposes, not only on our judgment of specific actions.

The Hebrews were reminded in the Ten Commandments, (Exodus 20:16) not to bare false witness or testimony about another. That commandment is necessary because people often ruin the reputation of others by what they say. Our tendency to become more involved in hearsay or outright lying means were need more than one perspective to find where truth lies. Truth and justice go hand in hand. God's people should be special sources of refuge from oppression. Economic justice sets the tone for much of the rest of society's structures for justice. God's people must help one another economically instead of taking advantage of other's needs. Respect for human dignity must be shown to all people even when we have legal claims against them. Punishment should fit the crime, with the human dignity of the criminal kept in mind. Those who appear to have insignificant, behind the scenes jobs could be fulfilling as heavy a responsibility as those more prominent.

Grace and generosity are facets of justice. Not every appearance of acting justly issues forth in justice as in II Samuel 15:3-6. A nation must not neglect setting up court systems for its people. The people must not too eagerly follow every voice calling for reform. Compassion and wisdom are bound up with justice. No human can rule wisely and justly without wisdom from God and humble dependence on God. Justice depends on the fair and wise use of power by political leaders. Leaders who manipulate and destroy others to satisfy personal greed stand under God's judgment. Justice depends on fair execution of the Law.

Personal vengeance cannot be tolerated in a society seeking justice. Society needs to listen to wise counsel of experience rather than the ambitious impatience of youth. God is good. His justice will be done. Eliphaz was correct in his statement about God, who is the ultimate hope of the poor and oppressed. (Job 5:3-7, 16) Job voiced strong confidence in the justice of God. If he could just present his case to God, he would be vindicated; for God always knows and does what is right. God cannot be deceived by the accusations of people like Job's friends. Job did not seek to be proven right so much as to stand the cause of his problems. He believed a just God knew that cause and would show it to him. (Job 13:3-14:17) Eliphaz declared that God is just and no sinner will escape His judgment. Again he had proper theology, but his application of a doctrine to the specific case of Job did not mean Job was the sinner who would not escape judgment (Job 15:17-35). Job did not understand why his troubles had come upon him, but he trusted in the justice of God. He wanted his appointed time for a legal hearing with God so that divine justice could be established and understood. Biblical justice exhibits a bias toward the weak and poor. One who acts upon it will take on the cause of those unable to defend themselves. Job's action challenges us to go beyond superficial compassion to action that attacks suffering and wrong. Job realized that God would act on any injustice he might commit.

It is wrong to oppress the weak or to use personal reputation and influence to manipulate the court system. The wise person knows that society often turns on us and denies us justice, but God still administers justice. We can call on him to help when all earthly hope fails. Inherent in the office of the civil leader is the responsibility for delivering the oppressed and using power for justice. God's people need to pray for leaders to have courage to establish justice. All human beings in God's creation are responsible to use power and position to help the needy and to establish justice. The psalmist in Psalm 94:1-23, encourages us with his sense of hope that God's relief will come. He is the supreme judge and is constantly aware of oppression and injustice. God's character and ways on behalf of the down and out are well known; we can trust His help. Those who are God's people will surely act as He does. People who do not act like God reveal some of their true character. God works for the oppressed, those for whom no one else will speak. The expectation is that people who call themselves after God's name will also execute justice. The courtroom is of all places expected to uphold integrity. Unfair decisions, bribery, punishment of the innocent, and persecution of just officials have no place in society. The ministry of the Messiah, (Isaiah 11:3-5) will be marked by His aggressive justice and righteousness on behalf of the needy. What human rulers or leaders and systems have not achieved, God's Messiah will. God's chosen servant has one mission, to establish international justice. Jesus took up His messianic mission, (Matthew 12:18-21). He expects His disciples to dedicate themselves to the same ministry. God's

Dr. Gilbert Edwards

design for His world is eternal justice and righteousness for all people and nations.

An unjust people who think they can fool God faces His inevitable judgment. False religious leadership can support and promote injustice. Religious leaders must not be motivated by greed or ego needs. God established leaders of His people to create and maintain a just social order. When they become a problem, they face destruction. God looks for people who will stand in the gap between Him and His people to intercede for them and build up the wall of justice. Serving God must be top priority for a society seeking justice. Leaders from all areas of life can let greed destroy their value systems. Devotion to evil and disregard for the value of persons mark the end of justice and hope for a nation. God supplied justice and power to His faithful, courageous speakers to call society to renewal. Society must be built on God's requirements rather than on human ambitions.

What is the definition of biblical justice? Zechariah provides an excellent response. (Zechariah 7:8-10) It is mercy, compassion, and the bringing of balance into things gone wrong for widows, orphans, foreigners or the poor. These Old Testament categories translate into our own time as those who are the vulnerable people of society, those who have no one to speak for them. Justice begins as an attitude of love in the heart. This expresses itself in actions defending those whom society easily defrauds. A mark of the Spirit within us is a hunger to live out the will of God. Without God's energizing, sustaining and closeness, our fulfillment in life grows weak. By feeding on His presence and guidance, our lives grow and mature. Seeking the will of God causes us to be at cross purposes with our cultural values. Our call is not to be religious experts, but humble servants of God's justice. God's people cannot achieve a just society simply through human zeal and enthusiasm. We must receive righteousness from God through faith. Proclaiming the gospel should lead to a transformed people who can be a transformed society. God is a just God. His righteousness is ever true. He will not let the right fail. Nor will He let evil continue. He is faithful to His own righteous nature and will set all things right in the end. We should fall down in worship and gratitude.

## Christian Ethics in Relation to War and Peace

War and conflict are as ancient as humanity. For ages, people have acted upon the conciliatory impulses of God to seek peace. The distribution of goods and wealth is a major area of dispute leading to conflict. The willingness to compromise even to the extent of giving up economic advantages often leads to peace. Political domination often leads to dissatisfaction and rebellion. The Bible often describes rebellion and war as facts of human life without making a moral judgment concerning their justification or their evil character. The human struggle over limited natural resources leads to conflict and at times, to war. Compromise and refusal to demand one's rights can lead to peace. Marriage and sexual relationships may lead to conflict which erupt into war. Individual agreements should lead to peace, but human greed and vengeance leads to violation of agreements and war. Our goals should not be to satisfy our greed or gain absolute justice for ourselves. Our goal should be to reach satisfactory agreements of peace and to abide by them.

Persons dedicated to anger, war and violence do not receive blessings. Improper human attitudes are the basic cause of war. God's might enters into the conflict of this world on the side of right and justice. What justifies retaliation? To what extent does God allow self-defense? This passage, Exodus 17:8-16, shows one instance where God opposed retaliation. Only an obedient people can expect God's protection from enemies.

The Bible speaks of God using human warfare, (Exodus 23:22-33) to establish His purposes for His people. It does not thereby justify any people who call themselves God's people entering into war, demanding and expecting God to fight for them. The Bible speaks of God's initiative, not human initiative. God's presence provides protection for His people, but the goal is rest from war, not domination through war. War is not a godly goal. We must not use self-interest to provoke others to war. Peace not war is the ideal of God for His people. Fighting in a Christian home is not allowed.

Some limits must be imposed upon war efforts; otherwise, the results will be so barbaric as to render society worse after the war than before. The wrong use of international politics too often leads to war and fosters enemies. Joshua's was (Joshua 10:1-43) unique. God was directly involved in fighting for His people. Good's military involvement in the Exodus and conquest, (Exodus 15:3-10) established His chosen people and displayed His unique divine power before the nations. Contemporary war does not involve this one-time divine purpose or direct divine involvement. God remains the sovereign Lord of history who can accomplish His will through the political and military actions of the nations. Obedience was the key for Joshua's war. Israel won because Joshua obeyed God perfectly. The call to warfare no longer rings out from God to us. The call to obedience does peace, not war, is the climax of Joshua. Rest from war, not continued involvement in fighting, is God's continuing will for His people. His people can enjoy peace because God fulfills His promise. The Hebrews, (Judges 5:8) had lost the spiritual warfare taking place as they accepted other gods. The moral erosion that followed could not be combated because no strength physical nor spiritual was available. Biblical warfare was always tied to God's redemptive plans and His people's spiritual faithfulness. Gideon's victory, (Judges 7:1-25) stirs every generation of believers to realize that their ultimate strength for life comes from God. A people using their resources to their limits and being steadfast in the application of them, can find victory in all of life's fights. Courage and perseverance mixed with faith in God led to the demise of the Midianites. The victory was ultimately God's doing in that neither Gideon nor his men ever had to strike a blow. Treaties are the proper way to solve conflict; war is not. Treaties must be fair to both sides. Unjust treaties do not settle conflicts; they create more. God is on the side of persons suffering injustice. No human power has the right to disobey God. God can turn victory into defeat for a disobedient people.

War is not a place to build a personal reputation, consolidate personal power and then oppose God. All of us are vulnerable to rising quickly and then allowing that fame to displace our since of obedience to God. God can become the enemy of His one-time hero. We can never gain enough power to oppose God. The account in Kings 6:8-23, demonstrates the themes of mercy, peace and reconciliation with one's enemies that were a part of the Hebrew theological tradition. Israel engaged in the political conflicts of that time, but Israel knew God's will was peace, rest and mediation of conflict. War is not always an option to settle differences. Uzziah exhibited model behavior in his covenant with God until his pride got the best of him (II Chronicles 26:6-22). He evidently determined he could rule without God's help. Making that situation worse, Uzziah tried to take over priestly functions, too. Such a swing of attitudes called forth the judgment of God.

Though the Hebrews were often warlike (Psalms 20:7-8), they knew their ultimate source of power and might came from God. Any military advantage they might have had was not enough, if their disposition toward God was improper. Those who are not at peace with themselves, or with God will exhibit his war likeness (Psalms 55:20-21); however, cleverly hidden by actions and words to others. War can end only when it ends in human hearts. Peace must be more than the absence of international conflict. It includes prosperity, life and justice for all people. Contrasting the intent, loyalties and actions of persons distinguishes peace lovers from peace despisers (Proverbs 12:20).

International war grows out of personal strife. Such strife roots in insecure people who mock the achievements of others and in jealousy fight for undeserved attention. Society begins the road to peace when it helps these people change their ways. Righteousness and peace have an intimate relationship. The presence of righteousness more than implies peace. Peace is the work of God's spirit establishing justice among people and leading people to act rightly toward one another. Peace will bring security, confidence, and freedom from danger and adequate resources. Obedience to God's ethical imperatives is integrally tried to the results of peace. Peace is more than empty words and false promises. Peace can only come when God's people live peaceably with one another instead of imitating the world. Happy, satisfied and fulfilled will be the one who works for and does the things that make for peace (Matthew 5:9). The way of the peacemaker is not a weak kneed approach to life, but it is a way of courage. It transcends the world's attitudes and methodologies of bringing change. It makes God's moral teaching the center of community life and seeks to replace weapons of war with tools which will provide basic needs for all the world's population.

## Christian Ethics in Relation to Language

Misuse of God's name is more than profanity. Misuse includes the profane life-style of a child of God. We who bear God's name must not give other people reason to lose respect for His name. A word spoken cannot be called back, whether a word of truth or falsehood. Anger must be expressed in appropriate ways. Misusing God's name or asking for God's curse on a person are not appropriate expressions. To curse a leader or a people is to ask God to destroy a system He established to provide justice.

Language properly used is related to justice. Failure to admit we have found lost property makes us guilty of lying and theft. It is worth taking notice that language used to refer to God is the most serious and important communication we make. God does not want us to use His Holy name to bring curses on our enemies.

Isaiah articulated God's opinion against language which indicated a prideful spirit (II Kings 19:22-23). Though we throw insults at other people, our attitude is ultimately one which insults God. God hates those attitudes of deceit and greediness, which our language expresses as we ridicule and condemn others. Job's discipline of his tongue (Job 27:4), exemplified a profound test of character. Our words indicate our goals. If we want to bring peace and good to the world, we must not speak evil or lie about other people. What and how we say things is an indicator of our true spirit. God's judgment is lodged against speech, which does not exemplify love of neighbor. Our religious talk is only as good as our ethical actions. The same words used in different ways may represent different ethical problems and perspectives. These verses in Psalms 69:22-28, are spoken to the enemy with intention to bring the descriptions to pass would represent cursing, hatred, vengeance, anger and the desire to kill. Our tongue can get us into trouble. Sometimes we speak without taking time to think. We may agree without thinking to a contract made by a dishonest person. When we recognize the wrongness of our attitudes and works, we need to act immediately. We must not quit until we are reconciled to the other person and nullify the agreement. In so doing we must admit our wrongness. Loose treatment of the power of words can erode friendship or even lead to the destruction of a nation. Learn the secret of silence; try to be silent.

Words can hurt or heal. Wise use of the power of words leads us to know the importance of timing, both knowing when to speak and when to listen. Language backed by the integrity of the speaker builds confidence and leaves lasting results. Talk, no matter how spiritual its application, must be backed by action. Words without work lead to the spiritual poorhouse. Language communicates our emotions and our intellect. In so doing, it attracts or repels people. The company we keep feeds our tongue. We will communicate to people what we listen to. Eventually, we usually believe and become what we constantly hear. We must know the question before we give the answer. The power of the tongue to sway is awesome. One who realizes that and uses the tongue rightly, will enjoy a rich meaningful life. Our use of language should be productive, helping us reach our goals. Leaders, if you love truth and know how to communicate truth, tactfully you will have many supporters. A message appropriately delivered can lift our spirit. One who boasts actually declares his emptiness of spirit. Unfulfilled words wear us out; good news refreshes us. To falsely convict a person of crime is to fight a war against our neighbor. The careful listener recognizes a foolish speaker. It is a losing battle to attempt to engage such people on their level. The mature person in God attempts to raise the level of conversation and to guide the fool away from foolish conceit. Making jokes at another's expense shows foolishness. Playing on another's emotions, and intentions is dishonest and malicious. We need to find better way to gain attention. How do we treat gossip? We are not to give it credence be ever responding to it. Such approach will soon see the end of gossip and cause us to avoid fights with other persons.

Language can deceive for a while. We need to refuse to trust charmers whose heats oppose their lips. Charming lies can ruin the speaker and other people. Eventually, the charmer is found out. We need to resist all temptations to speak anything but the truth. We need to be cordial and tactful in confronting others, but we need to face differences honestly. In the long run, confrontation gains more respect than saying simply what the other wants to hear. Cautious use of language is necessary to succeed in any area of life. Constant speaking without thinking or listening leads nowhere. Insincere and malicious ideas get communicated to those whom we should want to be the very last to hear. Out words should reveal thoughts that are pure and truthful. Can one win by deceit? Yes, but it will finally be brought to judgment because lying reflects broken relationships with God and other people.

Society is the loser when lying, deceit, mistrust, slander and enmity rules its tongue. We should exhibit such integrity of character that we do not have to make any kind of vow indicating our truthfulness. People should be able to take any word we say at face value. Lying has no place among God's people. Neither does nagging criticism that seeks to divide God's church. Words that do not strengthen church fellowship should never be uttered. Language and speech are good gifts of God. Rather than foolish use of these gifts or using our speech to injure others, Christians are admonished to use their speech as a means of communicating their gratitude to God for His gifts of life to us. We never have reason to use obscene language or jokes. We must find better ways to satisfy our ego needs for importance.

Being righteous is much more important than being coarsely funny. A person ruled by Jesus Christ and led by the spirit will put away speech patterns reflecting anger and defamation of others' character. Words need to please God, not impress other people. We can ruin our reputation and our contribution to other people with a few ill-chosen words. Satan delights in controlling our tongue. We have no power over the tongue unless we submit it totally to God. Nothing should escape our mouths that is not praise to God in some way. Christian lips should not harm other people even after having suffered insults. Love, honesty, peace, blessings and prayer should mark the Christian language. Gossip seeks to destroy another person in order to gain power, position, prestige or personal attention. End time tribulation will lead many to blasphemy rather than repentance.

## Christian Ethics in Relation to Alcohol

The ugly side of the use of alcohol became apparent early in human existence. (Genesis 9:21) Drunkenness allows a person to be manipulated by other persons for their selfish interests. No purpose justifies intoxicating and manipulating another person. Alcohol robs people of the capacity to make decisions and judgments. Biblical law does not tolerate drunkenness behavior (Deuteronomy 21:20), but society often condones or even affirms drunkenness.

When this occurs, society sets up an example for new generations to follow which eventually may lead the society to ruin. Christians should work to discourage drunkenness in every way. Proverbs 20:1, expresses consciousness of the dangers inherent in wine. Wise people do not give alcoholic drinks the opportunity to control their mind and take away their wisdom. They do not want to become silly braggarts and stupid brawlers.

> Proverbs 23:20, 29-35 – these verses seem to have been written to worn abusers of strong drink and of the consequences they face; quarreling, fights, injuries, ugly physical appearance, confused minds, separation from reality, dangerous loss of feeling, drowsiness and addiction.

> Isaiah 5:11-12 – these verses pronounce judgment on those who have sought ultimate value for their lives in strong drink.

Alcohol makes us forget what God has done for us and so distorts our moral perceptions. We do not realize we stand under divine judgment. Being a drunkard and/or alcoholic is not the unforgiveable sin. It does involve sin of which one must repent to be part of God's kingdom just as we must repent of all other sin. Sinful habits are not part of the Christian life.

Paul talked about avid drunkenness (Ephesians 5:18), for all sorts of other evils could follow. Rather than being deceived about being euphoric through wine, Paul exhorts us to know true euphoria through a life fulfilled by the Holy Spirit. Leaders must set example for other to follow. Getting drunk is not excusable for a leader. Older women play an influential role in the Christian community and must teach by good example, as well as words. They also should not be addicted to alcohol. Women's substance abuse can have a deadly effect on a new generation.

## Christian Ethics in Relation to Property Rights

God cares for His children. He knows our material needs. The wicked of this world may have more of its goods than the righteous, but in the perspective of eternity the righteous are better off. Being on God's side is better than being rich. In our natural state, the God created desire for order and creativity are perverted into covetousness and greed. Without the guidance of God's perspective regarding the reasons why we have material things and how we can use those, we are aimless wonderers to collect wealth for no good purpose is meaningless.

A proper relationship with God leads a person to give proper priority to other concerns. Family life and economic relationships will reflect a sense of stewardship and responsibility. Though literal accumulation of wealth may not follow, the quality of one's life will reflect the true wealth of fulfillment and righteousness. In Psalms 144:12-15, it states that security and love of family, fulfillment and accomplishment in one's work, peace and protection for the community, and economic security reflect God's blessings.

Wisdom is knowing the way of the Lord. Wisdom comes through experience with God in His world, and includes experiencing His discipline. Worth more than any material value we can place on it, wisdom causes us to have the upward look toward God and outward look toward our neighbor. Without wisdom, material goods tempt us to look only toward ourselves. Material goods cannot buy a pleasant life of peace. Wisdom puts peace as our top priority-in our life with God.

Choosing to seek and follow God's wisdom lets us see wealth in proper perspective. So seeking wealth does not become the all-consuming goal of life. Gaining wealth should not become an end in itself. This effort does not provide the godly person a reason to be lazy and not work. Wisdom leads us to work by which we reap material security. Dishonesty is the opposite of the character traits God calls for and honors; justice, mercy, loving-kindness and righteousness. If we use dishonesty to supply material needs, we need to ask God for wisdom to put life back in perspective.

Wealth is not the final good; it carries potentially devastating power for character. It cannot satisfy the claim for righteousness demanded by God and fulfilled only through a faith relationship in this life. Neither can it provide safety from God's judgment. Even in this life a good salary does not purchase life's truly basic needs. Wealth may pay the ransom when greedy persons threaten us. Righteous people without wealth do not have to endure such threats. What has wealth really purchased?

Material greed has destructive implications not only for one's self, but also for all other relationships. Property is never more valuable than people. Duty to family reputation and needs for outweigh any responsibility to gain material goods. Some friends last only as long as one has money to spend on them. Proper relatedness to God teaches us that the true value of people is not to be measured in how much they have, or do not have materially. Poverty is not a value to be set as life's goal, but neither is wealth.

Indebtedness is a kind of slavery, over extension of credit without an appropriate repayment agreement can mean loss of one's possessions, one's reputation, and if a constant theme of life, loss of one's integrity. To become rich and exercise oppressive rule over the helpless poor is not the goal of life. Wealth for its own sake is deceptive in its promise of satisfaction. It leads to loss of personal integrity and values serving the rich and powerful, to fleeting success with riches which do not provide the emotional and spiritual riches we seek, or to deception and dishonesty. A wise person learns the limits of material needs and lives within those rather than constantly responding to the drive of personal wants, which are never satisfied. The stingy rich show by their actions where their hearts are. They care little for those without material things. They reveal little true wisdom poverty of spirit awaits them, even though they may amass a fortune. Only generous, giving persons are truly rich.

Honesty and satisfaction are basic values leading to the good life. Daily bread, not assured luxurious retirement is what we should ask of God. Envy's appetite will never be satisfied. It provides proper motive for no undertaking. Ecclesiastic gives a true testimony of one who has recognized the true source of his wealth, the satisfaction of a job well done, and the proper use of the good gifts of God. God's displeasure and judgment will be revealed against those who have accrued property at the expense of others. They have become ostentatiously rich through the injustice imposed on those who have little. The rich are often guilty of economic injustice. Rather than defend the widows, orphans or poor as God expects, they became rich off of them (Exodus 22:21; Deuteronomy 10:18; 27:19). Jeremiah 17:11, states that utter folly of depending on material wealth for soul sustenance, personal wealth gained by making others suffer is worthless. One who practices corrupt economic practices against the poor and needy does not show a living relationship with God. Sometimes only tragedy and crisis can teach the true value of material things. It took a time of judgment (Lamentations 4:1-2), for the people of Israel to recognize the folly of trusting in gold and gems for their sense of security. The prophetic warnings against their oppressive economic practices came true. Ezekiel 22:12, 27-29, states the horrible enumeration of economic injustices and abridgement of human rights, the signs of getting God's ways are seen in overcharging, extortion, oppression of the poor and the denial of justice to those who have no advocate. Attitude changes and the actions which match are the signs of God working in one's inner being. Too often our ease and comfort veil us from seeing economic injustice in our world. Our actions show we think if all is well with us, all must be well with everyone else. Our complacency is no excuse for not grieving over injustice to others. Amos explains in chapter 8:4-6 that a sad time had come when the Sabbath held no respect by the people. They could hardly wait to get back to their economic exploitation.

Some people would put their faith in the created matter (money, gold, silver) rather than the God (the creator of this matter). The father of lies will use the same approach on us as he did with Jesus. The creation is God's, not the devil. Gaining the world and all its wealth is not a goal for Christians. (Matthew 4:8-9) Material needs are reality of life all people face. Jesus took our needs seriously and devoted much time to talking about them. (Matthew 6:19-34)

Material things are not bad in themselves. They become bad when we place more importance on them than on our relationship with God. Wealth can rob us of eternal hope with God. The person devoted to riches cannot respond to Jesus' call to the cross. Placing material things over personal relationships has disastrous results. One can become consumed by the bigger is better syndrome. Greed gradually gains control. All energy is expended on material security to that a vision of wealth guides character formation. Life is too short to be centered on the material.

God offers so many possibilities for us that it is foolish to spend all our physical and emotional energies on satisfying ego needs to have more than others. Let's look at Luke 15:11-32 – the Father's generosity seems whimsical to our contemporary minds. Yet such response to the son both before he left home and his return typifies God's grace toward us. In turn, unlike the elder brother we are to extend grace to others because we have been graced. Material goods serve best when they are shared in celebration of the renewal of human lives.

Money is a means to other ends, and not an end in itself. It should be used to establish relationships with people rather than for the accumulation of things. It must be used to display our honesty and trustworthiness. Riches do not absolutely shut the rich out of God's kingdom, but they do blind us to God's values. Riches too often replace God in a person's life. When they do, entry to God's kingdom is blocked. Thievery is wrong. (Exodus 20:15) Thievery in the name of religion and charity shows greed has consumed a life (John 12:4-6).

The Early Church – the gospel message led the first church to ignore personal property claims in the interest of meeting the needs of others (Acts 2:44-45). Greed and love of money may lead to tyranny and oppression of others. Christians seek to free people from such tyranny even when it brings persecution. In a sense, everyone to whom we owe a monetary debt owns a part of our allegiance. Such allegiances can be so burdensome as to draw us from our first love of Jesus Christ. Greed is contagious. Association with greedy people willing to swindle others brings the growing temptation to reach their financial class and use their methods. Greed and swindling are as evil as sexual immorality, drunkenness, slander and idolatry. The Christian calling includes the imperative of seeking honest ways of making a living. The goals in our work are to protect a witness for Jesus Christ as well as to share of one's earnings with those who have little of this world's material goods. The world's richest person was Jesus, who stated that He had no place to lay His head (Matthew 8:20). He shared the Heavenly Father's unlimited resources. Greed is a form of idolatry, making what is material take the place of God. Many who consider themselves wise in money matters count or will not count the costs involved in pursuing money as an end in itself.

Once entered, the trap of greed is a difficult one from which to escape. Too often money becomes the chief goal of religious teachers who become willing to teach or preach any kind of false doctrine and stir up trouble in churches simple to make money. People rich in material goods should not be declared guilty of greed because of association. No everyone is called to a life of poverty. How would the Kingdom of

God advance sometimes without the necessity of funds? Those entrusted with riches are warned to make sure their priorities do not shift away from primary loyalty to God, to primary loyalty to money. They need to check their attitude towards other people, their generosity with the needy, and the richness of their actions in light of God's will. Some of the slickest hucksters in the world are those who prey on unsuspecting people by means of a religious message for a price. Such practices call us to remember the gospel is free. People pursue material goods as ends in themselves, but these things have nothing of the eternally permanent about them.

Humility is the only attitude proper for the rich. The poor suffer oppression, injustice, and ridicule at the hands of the rich. We are to treat the rich with love as any other person, but favoritism shown for the rich is a sin. James 2:1-18, states that the credibility of one's relationship with God can be perceived through one's treatment of the poor meeting for worship and Bible study, even at the work places are central to church life. Such meetings are open to all people with favoritism shown to none. Our attitude to and actions with property reflects our love for and relationship with Christ. True love acts to help the one in need. Helping others is the business of the people of God. Wealth cannot be measured in material terms. People under persecution and poverty are rich if they hold fast to faith in Jesus Christ.

Wealth is deceiving. We may not have what we think we possess. God is the only source of true wealth. The last days will reveal the nature of true wealth, leaving many in mourning because earthly treasures were the only wealth they knew (Revelation 18:9-20).

*Dr. Gilbert Edwards*

## Christian Ethics in Relation to Social Order and Social Relationships

As a portion of the holiness code (Leviticus 19:1-8), these ethical expectations are based on God's holiness. God's people are to be holy like God, not sinful like the nations. Horizontal relationships with our fellow human beings must reflect our vertical relationship with God. Picking and choosing is not an alternative for God's people as we make moral choices. We must obey all God's commands and remain within all the limits He sets. The criterion is what we like or agree with, but it's what He say.

Lower moral standards give cause for rejection from society and from God's people. We are different from all other parts of society; we are God's holy people. Religious leaders of their special responsibilities should be reminded. Any misconduct on their part brings dishonor on God's name and leaves God's people to ignore God's holiness. Christian leaders should serve only because God has set them apart to obey Him in all aspects of life.

Society must have guidelines for ongoing order. God's people provide a continuing witness through their ongoing practices. The rhythm of the calendar must provide time to work and time to celebrate the fruits of our labor which God provides. One who lives a godly life can expect generally a peaceable life. One goal of God's commands and moral limits is to establish a safe, peaceful social order. God's covenant regulations set up a way of life leading to security and peace. God wanted the best life for His people. Such blessings (Leviticus 26:3-13), could only come to those who obey Him. Refusing God's moral limits invited cursing and

46

disrupting of the social order. (Leviticus 26:14-45) Moral relationships involve personal communication and response between God and His people. When God acts in response to disobedience, He seeks to lead us back to obedience. He calls us to maintain social order. Responsibility is the keystone of social order (Numbers 30:1-2). We must be able to trust a person to carry out commitments.

The social order must protect members from rash vows they feel forced to make, or which they make without proper understanding of circumstances. God's laws establish an order most outsiders recognize as wise and desirable. (Deuteronomy 4:1-8) They meet all standards of righteousness. People have no reason to criticize or change God's social order. God's social order is set up to prevent want and need among His people. Full obedience by His people should lead to divine blessings which would eliminate poverty. People who do not fully obey cannot demand or expect such blessings. The ethical cohesiveness of a community depends upon mutual respect and care of property. We must respect and restore property belonging to others. God wants to bless His people. Blessings take many forms as God works personally with us. Curses replace blessings when we forsake God and refuse to repent. No one, no matter how powerful or prestigious has the right to take another human being's personal pleasure (II Samuel 12:7-14).

Business relationships often categorize and separate people. Paul did not comment on the rightness or wrongness of the institution of slavery (Philemon 15-17). Instead, he provided a basis for overcoming the social barriers of business relationships and ultimately of doing away with slavery. Christian purity comes through the truth of faith in Jesus Christ. It expresses itself in love for others. Consistent hatred of others is not the trait of a Christian. Love should characterize the Christian's relationships with other people.

Relationships, not rules, are at the heart of Christian ethics. Love is the root of right relationships. Love is not something we manufacture. Love is the central characteristic of God Himself, and therefore, is a gift we receive from Him. Love is defined, not by words, but by the act of God in giving His son to die on the cross for us. That love compels us to love others. When we do, we show we belong to God and He lives in us.

## Christian Ethics in Relation to Murder

Exodus 20:13, forms the central reference point regarding the sacredness of life in the Old Testament. The major emphasis of the commandment is that life is a gift from God and its stewardship is to be guarded carefully. Though generally the application is that there should be no vengeful killing (murder), the statement still puts the burden of proof upon anyone who takes another's life in whatever circumstances. To take life away from another lightly was perceived as an attempt at taking the place of God s controller of life. Accident killing differs from murder and must be dealt with through different processes of the legal system. Murder is so serious a crime that the Bible sets up the death penalty as the proper legal response. (Exodus 21:12-14) Intention plays a strong role in biblical ethics. Justice is decided on a person's attitude and purposes, not only on our judgment of specific actions.

In a world dominated by cause and effect values, little time was given to reconciliation or rehabilitation. Therefore, often the murders associated with political intrigue, war and interpersonal conflict do not reflect normative, timeless principles for dealing with injustice. Caution must be applied before making quick jumps of application to contemporary time based on such incidents. Such caution asks from where the initiative comes, for any acts of killing. Arranging another's death is murder as much as actually committing the crime. God condemns such action. No one has the right to take another's life neither vengeance, nor political ambition. Justifying the plotting and murdering of another person or assassination is wrong. Done in the guise of friendship, it becomes even more abominable. Even the violence of warfare should be controlled by concern for human welfare. God condemns persons who violate all common understandings of fair treatment to anyone. Wicked people cannot stand the presence of righteous people. The righteous become murder victims because their presence is witness to the guilt of the wicked. The physical act of taking a life is a grievous thing. Rather than limiting the fulfillment of moral law to outward conformity, Jesus located the root of murder at the attitude level. (Matthew 5:21-22) Such a perspective should lead the contemporary Christian to give special attention to those attitudes which may cause actions hurtful to others, whether physically, emotionally or socially. Such discipline of character takes seriously the sanctity and quality of life. For Christians murder is an attitude. It arises from guilt and envy and goes on to hatred. Harboring hatred is murder even if no physical act is committed. We avoid murderous hatred through letting Jesus Christ's love live in us (I John 3:11-15). Murder leads to eternal judgment, punishment and separation from God. (Revelation 21:8)

## Christian Ethics in Relation to Righteousness

Relationship with God promises a clearer sense of the way to go in life as God provides light for that life. The righteous person is one on God's pathway of life. Marks of righteousness are those actions which reflect perseverance, courage, compassion, consistency, integrity, peace, joy and a sense of what is appropriate. Cruelty characterizes the wicked; kindness characterizes the righteous.

Righteousness is more than an individual characteristic. It is a necessity for nations to survive. Those who choose righteousness over wickedness can be assured of the presence and protection of God (Proverbs 15:9). One who has sought the life of righteousness will reflect that righteousness in old age. Work for good and justice. The results will allow others more possibilities for doing the works of justice. Wicked advisors can destroy a person. Wickedness generates fear; righteousness brings joy. The wicked and righteous do not mix. They totally oppose each other. Joy and concern for the underprivileged characterizes righteous behavior. Justice and righteousness ultimately belong to God. In Him we find the power to restore these characteristics where they once were found in a society. He seeks to establish a people in right relationship with Him and seeks to ensure fair treatment for all people. Murder, trickery, deceit, theft, bribery and unjust courts mark a nation as God's enemy. Obedience to God is rewarded individually and socially in the fruit of justice and righteousness.

To be God's people is to worship Him and to pursue right actions which give stability to society. When God achieves His goal of a righteous people, tyrants will no longer rule so terror and terrorism will vanish. Impatient people must let God fulfill His promises His way. We may give up on our dream of a righteous people. God will not be silent forever. He will act in righteousness to save His people and display their righteousness to the nations (Isaiah 62:1-2)

The apocalyptic vision and the history (Daniel 9:29) to which its points have an ethical goal. God seeks to inform, ensure and motivate His people by revealing His eternal purpose of establishing eternal righteousness. Apocalyptic is a call to be a faithful citizen of God's eternal Kingdom of righteousness. Righteousness and justice sowed in the name of God will bear its fruit in due time. God's people cannot wait passively for His salvation. They must act in ways to give stability and hope to society. In His time God will act righteously to save us. God's righteous ones can be recognized by their pattern of life. Human righteousness reflects God's character. By undergoing the act of baptism, Jesus demonstrated His commitment toward the work of God's Kingdom. Such public professions solidifies our resolve toward Christian action and represent one of the righteous acts God's people can do. Jesus was the righteous messiah (Matthew 3:150.

Righteousness is not a self-satisfied attitude of a religious elite. Self-proclaimed righteous people may be so set in their opposition to God's ways that Jesus Christ's message cannot teach them. Righteousness involves honoring and ministering to God's righteous people. Present circumstances may indicate that righteousness is foolish and unrewarding. Ultimately, the righteous will receive their just rewards (Matthew13:43). Attitudes shape actions. Over a period of time our actions will betray the hypocrisy and evil we harbor. Those whom Jesus Christ addressed prided themselves in outward pious actions, but their attitudes and goals were wicked. Judgment is certain for hypocrites who build their own reputations at any cost. They will have to endure God's vengeance for all the truly righteous people that these religious hypocrites persecuted and killed.

Through Jesus Christ's righteous act we are transformed, devoting our lives to the righteous way of life He pioneered. Therefore our lives mirror God's holiness, and we receive eternal life as God's gracious wage (Romans 6:15-22). Righteousness is protection against evil temptations. Unless we are slaves to righteousness, we will be slaves to Satan and sin (Romans 6:15-22). Righteousness is also a visible witness to those around us that life in God does not avoid the spiritual perils of this world, but rather engage them and defeat them.

Our righteousness comes through our faith in Jesus Christ, who as the sinless suffering servant, counts His righteousness as ours. This righteousness, like that portrayed in the Old Testament, is not static but is known for its application to personal and social behavior. Such faith and righteousness are difficult to separate since they move together in observable life style and conscious choice. We cannot be righteous in our own efforts apart from Jesus Christ. We cannot receive righteousness from Jesus Christ without faith. We cannot be counted as righteous in Jesus

Christ without the desire to let the Spirit create a life of righteous act in us. God is the standard of righteousness. Disciples are His born again children who imitate His actions by doing right (I John 2:29). God is righteous, meaning that He not only opposes what is evil but, is the source of what is right. He actively seeks to make His people righteous. Righteous lives show God at work.

Ethics center on knowing and doing the good. Human standards cannot define the good. Good is a personal characteristic of God which Christians imitate in their hearts. God's righteousness creates righteousness in those who come into a relationship with Him. Being in a relationship with God is more than an empty formality. If righteousness is not produced in the life of one who claims to be a believer, then that is a sign that one is not in a true relationship with God. The last judgment will reveal our true righteousness; all our deeds will lay open before God as He judges us (Revelation 20:11). The call to repentance will one day cease. Human intentions to change will never have another chance to become reality. Therefore, the apocalyptic calls us to repent and become holy like God before that day comes. In that day, people will not suddenly become righteous (Revelation 22:11).

The use of wisdom, understanding and knowledge to build intellect God is an intelligent God; it is seen in His creation. Seeing what God has done and understanding its meaning is two different things. Perception is not only intellectual, but also spiritual. We must be properly related to God to receive spiritual insight. Such insight leads us to see that the greatest knowledge is the knowledge and will to obey God. Wisdom is a gift from God. Wisdom involves literary and musical skills and factual knowledge. Its proper use attracts the attention of others.

<u>Intellect</u> is the faculty of reasoning and understanding objectively, especially with regard to abstract or academic matters. It's the understanding or mental powers of a particular person, an intelligent or intellectual person.

<u>Intelligence</u> is the ability to acquire and apply knowledge and skills. Wisdom and knowledge are the basic skills needed by a ruler or a person who leads.

Knowledge is not the private preserve of any individual. It is open to all. No one has any basis for assuming knowledge is reserved for one person while another remain ignorant. However, granting the availability of knowledge does not mean that everyone will appropriate it in the same way. The same God who give life also gives wisdom to his people. Just as much as life itself, intellectual attainments come from God's grace. A common human failing is talking about things of which we possess no knowledge; thus, distorting the understanding of others as well as parading our own ignorance. For all the great attainments of people, human ignorance of both life and death far outstrips human knowledge. Until we know the secrets of life and death, we have no basis to challenge God's justice or His control of the universe. As usual, the heart in the Old Testament is understood as the seat of the mind, the intellect and the will. Life should be so lived that people become wise as God intends. Only He can teach us to plan our lives and use our time in such a manner that we reach the full measure of wisdom He plans for us. Such wisdom leads us to accept the sorrows that life brings and to be grateful for the signs of God's love and care. The greatest human intellectual achievement, which he receives from the world system, are insignificant in comparison to God's wisdom. Only fools take so much pride in their knowledge and intelligence that they ignore God, His purpose and commands. Human intellect should lead people to remember and ponder the great acts of God. The wisest people ponder God's love and learn from the mistakes of others. Here in Psalms 111:10, the fear of the Lord refers to a reverential attitude which leads us to obey God's law and revelation. This relationship to Him and His revealed word, lets people find true wisdom. Such wisdom centers on obedience to God rather than demanding obedience to or acceptance of our opinions and knowledge. Human wisdom finds its basis in God's revelation. True knowledge and judgment come from the study of God's word and will, and not from human philosophy and reasoning. Human philosophy helps us understand life to that philosophy is built on trust in God and His revelation. Learning has many sources. Powerful humans build up ways to rule and control. Teachers study human traditions and use human reasoning to gain knowledge. Such wisdom used correctly can be good and helpful, but it needs to be secondary. Genuine wisdom comes from God and the study of His word. Our intellect's purpose is to build life, not facts. God's revelation is the place to begin intellectual development. We can build a disciplined and well-ordered life on that foundation.

God's wisdom is personified as calling to people (Proverbs 1:20-33), making herself available to all who will respond. Wisdom is the gift of God and has the ability to rescue people from evil choices and poor decisions. Those who accept His wisdom will find it a firm basis for understanding His revelation, as well as all of life's knowledge. God's wisdom is revealed as the basis of all great accomplishments of humanity. Its origin is seen in God and was His companion in creation and is the basis of His revelation. This divine wisdom is offered to all who know and admit their own ignorance.

People are expected to develop their wisdom to their highest potential. Those seeking to develop their wisdom and knowledge are willing to be open to the examination of themselves and others. This is the way of intellectual stimulation and growth. God has given people minds with the expectation that we will use them to evaluate everything we hear and see. We must decide for ourselves, not simply accept another's opinion blindly regardless of the position or education of the other person. Even a person who is a fool can have access to the wisdom of God. God does not have secret knowledge He wants to give only to a few. Wisdom is a far more lasting attainment than wealth (Proverbs 16:16). Words expose a person's ignorance quicker than silence (Proverbs 17:28). The search for wisdom is far more profitable than the search for wealth (Proverbs 19:8). An ingredient of wisdom is the recognition of personal intellectual need combined with the ability to accept and utilize education (Proverbs 19:20).

God's wisdom leads to self-discipline through the power of His spirit and the teaching of His word. Wisdom leads to careful planning for the future. The wise person learns from the experience of others. Genuine wisdom recognizes its own limitations and is ready to learn more. Self-centered pride robs us of the change to improve. Genuine friends in honest discussion sharpens the skill and wisdom of each other. We can never be so wise that we do not need to learn in dialogue with others of opposing viewpoints. God given wisdom alone brings joy (Ecclesiastes 2:26). Genuine wisdom is both life-giving and a refuge in the time of trouble (Ecclesiastes 7:11-12). The first step to attain wisdom is to recognize the folly of doing wrong. For all the greatness of human achievements, ultimate wisdom is still beyond human attainment. Only the eternal God knows everything. Human wisdom may enable persons to amass great pride; believing themselves to be beyond God's touch. God's judgment will show the weakness of such wisdom. Solving difficult problems involves honesty, admitting our limitations and seeking God's help. God can confound the wisest human. For all of humanity's intellectual accomplishments, the areas of ignorance still abound. (Daniel 5:7-9) Wise leaders admit the limits of their abilities and seek persons with the needed God given skills to solve problems. The ability to discern or perceive God's work comes from the wisdom which He alone imparts. God's wisdom helps people perceive that His way is the best way for us to live. Wisdom leads us to read God's inspired book and live by it. Humans make great plans and expect to accomplish them. We forget human intellect is always limited. We will never be wise enough to understand totally the will and purposes of God. Through His revelation, we can determine His will for our individual lives and the contribution we can make to the accomplishment of His universal purpose.

## Christian Ethics in Relation to Obedience

Two general ethical expectations (Genesis 17:1) on Abraham provided a basis for the specific expectation (Genesis 17:10). The pattern is the same for contemporary people of God. General principles for ethical decision making built on a covenant relationship gives direction for specific circumstances. Biblical ethics is founded in a covenant relationship that God initiated with His people. He promises salvation and expects obedience. The faithfulness of one generation leads to the renewal of the covenant with the next.

Developing our spiritual nature requires worship and obedience. Obey God's law, the Bible says, "Do not steal." The core attitude for stealing is coveting. The inner character damage done by coveting is severe. The society that God intends for His people is based on love for your neighbor, not envy. Thieves must make things right with the offended human party and with God. Theft is both a crime and a sin.

Be obedient to Deuteronomy 23:9-14, because personal hygiene is important. Certain basic practices leading to and maintaining good individual and corporate health should be implemented. Attention to positive physical and emotional health are marks of Christian character. Prayer will help you to be obedience to the will of God. Prayer is an exceedingly important ethical dynamic as it identifies pressing moral needs or issues before God. It solidifies resolve in the petitioner to address personal and social changes that should be made toward righteousness and is the beginning place for action for such changes to occur.

Obedience to God's standards, or law. In II Kings 23:3, Josiah represents an example of one in a leadership role who took seriously the matter of high personal and community standards. Because of the intensity and seriousness of his commitment to renewed application of God's standards for his life. Others followed is example. Our society, unlike Josiah's, is not one in which as the King does, so goes the community. Yet, ours is like Josiah's in that authenticity of word and life-style can be strong communications of God's truths. God permitted Satan to test Job's faith. Would Job be obedient to God if he lost his great wealth, his family and health? He was obedient and provided an example of obedience to all Jesus Christ's followers.

Obeying God means walking in His paths. It includes religious belief and the moral behavior accompanying that belief. In Ezekiel 11:18-21, it speaks of the new spirit and new heart brings with them a new obedience. Ezekiel's good news was that God would so renew His people that they would obey Him from the heart and not just the mind. Biblical ethics centers in the righteousness of God. Humans acknowledge our imperfect response to Gods known will and confess that God is perfect. God becomes the ethical standard rather than a list of rules and regulations. The Bible's laws and prophetic teachings reflect God's holy righteousness and provide guidelines for us to follow in seeking to be holy and righteous as He is.

When we are obedient to God good things happen. When Jonah finally obeyed God, the City of Nineveh repented. (Jonah 3:3-5) Our obedience can result in the salvation of others. Mary obeyed the Lord and became the mother of the world's Savior. (Luke 1:38, 74) Whenever we have to choose between obeying God and social authorities, we should obey God. Obeying God is not a dreaded, impossible duty, but a natural result of the Spirit in us. Paul, (Romans 7:6) contrasted the old way of life with the new way that Jesus Christ established. Since the old way was dominated by the law, he could be understood as saying Jesus Christ's way is not a way of moral obedience. To prevent this misunderstanding, he affirmed that Christians are set free from the law, just so we will be free to serve Jesus Christ by serving other people. Paul called this kind of service "the new way of the Spirit." The Spirit is not a passive observer of the lives of Christians. He is actively at work in all believers to transform us into the kind of person God wants us to be. This means new services in a new freedom with a fuller understanding (John 15:15).

The Spirit is not given for our enjoyment, but to change us so we will be of service to Jesus Christ. The Spirit pours God's love into our hearts. The Spirit produces the fruit of love in our lives, which leads us to be a better person. Obedient to God's moral imperatives is a strong witness to unbelievers. The powers of a holy life speaks for itself, for it speaks of God. To witness from any other perspective than a dedicated life puts lie to our words. We must live as well as speak, then the lost world can cling to no excuse for refusing God and His salvation. Obedience gives assurance of salvation. God's love is made complete in the life of the one who obeys God's commands. The life of the obedient disciple becomes a channel for God to express His redemptive love for others. If we do not obey God's commands, we can hardly have the confidence we know God through faith in Jesus Christ. John says that the person who claims to know

God but does not obey His commands is making a false claim. The reality of the world's end and God's judgment calls us to obedience and repentance. (Revelation 3:3)

In the face of the coming end of history, God's people are called to a new commitment to obedience, for only the obedient will be able to stand against the evil dragon (Revelation 12:7)

# CHAPTER IV

# THE DEVELOPMENT OF A BAD CONSCIENCE

When a person's moral consciousness is weak or undeveloped, innocent acts can appear wrong. If such a person commits that act, it has become a sin for that person and he or she is guilty. The act, although innocent to others, was done with the belief that it was wrong and, therefore, was an act of rebellion or disobedience against the conscience. However, it does not follow that an act is disobedient to scripture is justifiable whether or not anyone believes it to be correct.

Christians must accept one another's moral feelings, study scripture together to determine God's teachings, and tolerate differences in love. Divine commandments and the gift of freedom to choose whether or not to obey established the basis for the moral consciousness. Commands without the freedom to choose turn people into automations. Freedom without divine guidance provides the basis for an utterly unstable life and society.

Evil is frequently due to the human heart. Evil includes not only external public actions that oppose the will of God, but also internal secret intentions. The human moral will did not and does not improve with passing generations. Humans do not naturally choose to do good. We are more inclined to do evil.

In Psalm 1:1, this Hebrew word for blessing carries the idea of happiness indicating a state of pleasurable satisfaction. A life characterized by this emotion comes to those who avoid the path of sin. The Bible assumes everyone recognizes the path of descent into sinfulness through their own inner conscience. To avoid this path we must study God's teachings and fellowship with God's people. No one can plead ignorance to before God. He judges us on the moral knowledge we have those who know the teaching of God's word places judgment on that basis. Others have through creation a since to do right. They are judged on this basis. None can plead innocent.

All have sinned consciously against what they knew to be right. Right knowledge is not the criterion; right action is. Whether a person has knowledge of the word of God does not alone determine moral accountability before God. Many have sinned without knowledge of the word of God. Everyone has some internal code or law that acts as a standard of behavior. An expert in God's word can still be a sinner. God does not evaluate us on our knowledge of his will. He judges us because we disobey. We do not do what we know to do. The human conscience is not as sensitive to sin as God is. It is sin that makes a bad person. Because of that, we must change our minds and make it like Jesus Christ. Our moral consciousness may reveal sin (wrong-doing) and evoke guilt. If our conscience does not convict us of sin, we cannot claim innocence. We need to tune our consciousness to God's wave length concerning sin. Jesus Christ is the final judge who will reveal human motives. He has not called us to judge another person (I Corinthians 4:4-5). Paul's conscience (II Corinthians 2:12), would not let him carry out his plans. A person's conscience, while not naturally trustworthy, can be trusted when it is led not merely by human wisdom, but by the revelatory gift of God.

I Timothy warns us to watch out for the influence of deceiving and demonic spirits; the presence of false teachers who in hypocrisy and untruth forbid marriage and seek to impose food restrictions (I Timothy 4:1-3). The demonic teachers' consciences were so branded by evil that they lost all moral sensitivity and we no longer able to distinguish between right and wrong. This can happen to any person whose life has lost its foundation of faith. The conscience can confirm our moral and religious decisions if it has been cleansed by Jesus Christ.

Greed for money can corrupt us. True believers do not have to seek out secret teachings about eating and living habits. We are free to enjoy all of God's good creation without warning about ritualistic laws of cleanliness. Only corrupt persons need such laws because they have lost all moral sensitivity. The spiritual state of a person affects the sensitivity of the moral consciousness. The conscience cannot always be a trustworthy guide.

Peter states in Peter 3:16, to continue to keep a good conscience, which is moral goodness. The moral consciousness is not always pure (I Timothy 4:2). Christians in daily witnessing and living must continuously treat other people in such a way enemies will have no evidence to talk against us. Rather, enemies will be ashamed because of our good behavior. Life in this vein keeps the conscience clear. In the third chapter of the book of Genesis, it shows the beginning, the progress and the culmination of temptation and the consequence of sin. It depicts the earlies tragedy in the life of each human soul-the loss of man's happy, natural relation with God. Every man who knows his own heart, knows that the story is true; it is the story of his own fall. Adam is man and his story is ours.

There is an everlasting distinction between right and wrong, between good and evil. There have always been voices-serpent voices-deriding all moral do's and don'ts proclaiming instinct and inclination to be the trust guides to human happiness, and bluntly denying that any evil consequences follow defiance of God's commands. This chapter for all time works mankind against these insidious and fateful voices. In the words of Isaiah it seems to say, "Woe unto them that call evil good and good evil; that put darkness for light, and light for darkness; that put bitter for sweet and sweet for bitter! Woe unto them that are wise in their own eyes." The Ten Commandments that God gave to Moses, no religious document has exercised a greater influence or moral and social life of man than the divine proclamation of human duty known as, The Ten Commandments. These few brief commands cover the whole sphere of conduct, not only of outer actions, but also of the secret thoughts of the heart.

As I stated before a man conscience is not always good. If he had sin or did wrong, then he would have a guilty

*Dr. Gilbert Edwards*

conscience. In Old Testament time, to remove that guilt there must be a sacrifice offered, by presenting a sin or a guilt-offering unto God, The individual brought whenever a man's conscience prompted him to do so from a feeling of estrangement from God, in expiation of evil thoughts or unwitting sins (Job 1:5).

## Chapter V

# Educate Your Mind

The mind will have to be educated to characterize a good behavior, or show good conduct. Education is a basic task of the household. It should start building the mind at an early age, to produce better character. God wants every parent to teach their children at an early age. Deuteronomy 6:1-10, states that nurturing the faith of children through God-centered teaching is one of the greatest privileges of parenthood. It is also a sacred obligation. The task cannot be done on an occasional basis. It must be a continuous process-morning, noon and night. The word of God is to be quoted, explained, discussed, symbolized and written down. Most important, it is to be written upon the heart and incorporated into the parent's way of life so the children may have a daily example of godly living. The prayer of Manoah,

> "O Lord, I beg you, let the man of God you
> sent to us, come again to teach us how to
> bring up the boy who is to be born,"

models for all parents the need for God's guidance in the nurture and education of children. Whatever it takes to learn, we must do it. Job was willing to learn even from the criticisms of others (Job 6:24). This is the mark of a wise man. Only a fool assumes that his critics are always in the wrong. The godly person does not depend upon previous learning to keep walking in the way of the truth, but upon God's continued guidance.

The child of God never graduates from the school of divine instructions; every day is commencement. The Psalmist taught an important educational principle (Psalm 119:99-102) and only one who obeys the Word of the Lord can fully understand it. Divine truth is not something to be contemplated from a distance. It must be gripped within the arena of every day experiences. True wisdom depends upon obedience to God's percepts. If you really want to be educated, God is the starting point for the education that leads to wisdom. True knowledge, in the biblical sense is something more than a collection of factual information. It includes knowing how to conduct oneself in the practical affairs of everyday life, to make wise choices, and to have insight into the true nature of things. Wisdom of this kind can only grow out of an awareness of God and His purpose in the world.

Now back to the early stage of life, the first and most important classroom in the school of life is the home. Both father and mother are expected to assume responsibility for training and nurturing the minds of children. Though school and church might contribute significantly to the process of education, no outside agency can equal the influence of parents as an educative force. True wisdom promotes health, well-being, and happiness. Many of the problems that plague human existence springs from poor judgment, foolish choices and confused values. God-given wisdom helps us avoid these pitfalls and heightens the quality of life.

Instructions in the word of God and a serious commitment to live by it provides a safeguard against moral lapses. Wisdom is not confined to academic halls and classrooms. She walks the streets said Proverbs 8:1-7 and 11, moves among the people, and stands in crowded thoroughfares. Here is the biblical picture of the modern ideal of universal, lifelong learning, in which people can gain treasures of the mind and heart worth far more than material resources. God wants to teach us His ways through every experience of life. Long before modern educators learned of a predisposition toward learning, the biblical writer pointed out that a wise and knowledgeable person is receptive to further instruction. Learning kindles a desire for more learning (Proverbs 9:9). Parents must discipline children for the children to have a chance in life. Without discipline and correction we never learn. Watch who we imitate; we learn a great deal both good and bad, by imitating the behavior of others. This education principle is widely recognized by contemporary psychologists.

A hunger for knowledge is the mark of a wise person. Wisdom makes us understand our need for learning. The fool is a know-it-all; self-satisfied in ignorance. The biblical writer repeatedly emphasized the relationship between learning and the quality of being teachable. Just as children can learn from parental discipline, so can we learn from constructive criticism all through life, if we have the humility to accept corrective advice. The learner's self-discipline is more important than externally imposed discipline. The presence of good does not guarantee learning, for leaning is an active process in which learners seek truth and apply themselves to the task.

Indifference, self-sufficiency or dullness of mind and heart can close our ears to words of wisdom. We do not acquire knowledge by sitting passively and waiting for it. We must search for it as though it were a hidden treasure (Proverbs 22:17). We can fail to learn through indifference and apathy. Stubbornness can also stand as a barrier to learning often with disastrous results. Refusal to learn and change is a sin against God (Proverbs 29:1). In modern society, a man who has technical knowledge may be regarded to moral standards and practices.

In the scriptures, wisdom has a definite moral component. A person who has true wisdom does not associate with the wrong crowd or show other signs of moral illiteracy. In Prophet Isaiah's days he spoke about the divine teaching (which is the best teaching) being a major characteristic of the Messianic age (Isaiah 2:3; Jeremiah 31:33; Michah 4:2). As the Lord Himself instructs the people in His perfect law, justice, righteousness, harmony and universal peace will prevail. God's teaching in God's worship place should attract all people of all nations to Him. God has entrusted His people with His word to teach the people. Such teaching should lead people to faith. Don't make "fun" at the teacher's methods of teaching you, as the drunken priests were mocking Isaiah as they asked sarcastically, are you here to teach us, as though we were small children?" (Isaiah 28:9-10). In the process, they shed light on ancient Hebrew elementary education. Apparently, drill and repetition were important methods in the teaching of small children we need to learn to use the best technology to apply old and true methods of education. We must use whatever we can use to get better. A fundamental weakness in much religious instruction is that it comes a matter of mere words that make little difference to anyone.

The purpose of biblical teaching is to transform lives; not to pay lip service to verbal propositions. God wants obedience which comes from dedicated hearts, not just words falling from articulate lips. Beware of false teachers, they can corrupt your faith and undermine your ability to believe in the living God. The seed of false religious belief, planted in the mind can keep on growing through successive generations, by putting it into you and you putting it into some else. There are some people who are not teachable, or refuse to learn.

In Jeremiah 32:33, even when God Himself was their teacher, the children of Judah failed to learn. God's teaching included punishment and discipline for His people. Even divine discipline failed. What more forceful way to illustrate the necessity of learner's willing participation in the teaching-learning transaction? When we resist learning, no one can teach us. As in <u>Haggai 2:11-13</u> – God's people will always need teachers who can translate the written word of God into understanding for contemporary hearers.

Every teacher of the word of God has something in common with the Priests of Israel, who bore primary responsibility for teaching the people. As messengers of the Lord, God-called teachers are responsible for the accuracy and soundness of their instructions. When they carry out their teaching duties faithfully, they will have an impact on the behavior of individuals and on the moral standards of the community. Don't hide from learning; teaching is great. Teaching is what makes us better. We must be taught, it doesn't matter how old we are we can get better. Jesus taught, preached and healed. His salvation was perfectly balanced, providing for the whole person with spiritual, emotional and physical needs. He was known as "teacher". Teaching was His most characteristic function; whether in the synagogue, on a hillside or in the marketplace, everywhere He went He was called teacher. One of Jesus' greatest "subject" on teaching was widely known as <u>The Sermon on the Mount</u> – is actually depicted as a teaching situation. I look at it from the view of the "Beatitudes" – let this be your "attitude." Jesus and His disciples withdrew from the crowds, and Jesus assumed the familiar sitting posture of a teacher. Then He began teaching His followers. His teaching began with blessings on the way to happiness, not with commands (Matthew 5:2). As in the book of Matthew Jesus' disciples are teachers instructed in the love of the kingdom. As such, they combine the riches of their knowledge of Old Testament scripture with the new interpretations taught by the Master Jesus Christ. Christian teachers are constantly challenged to find new ways to communicate ageless truth, as each successive generation faces unique challenges. Jesus healing established the authority of His teaching What teacher do has a strong bearing on how people respond to what the teachers say. We need someone to teach us with authority as the Master Teacher, Jesus did.

Jesus began His public ministry with the activity that became His trademark – teaching. The synagogue was a logical place to do this since instruction was central to all synagogue services. The people were amazed that His interpretation were unique and original, for only Rabbis were permitted to teach with the authority conferred upon them by their masters (Mark 1:21, 22). Hypocritical teaching is worse than no teaching at all. Teachers who are pious on the outside, but corrupt on the inside can delude those who follow them leaving them worse off spiritually than they were before. Because teaching is an awesome responsibility, false teaching is a sin.

Good teachers are to help people. There should be a good method to teach people of how to be their best. Jesus used parables – parables were powerful teaching tools in the hands of the Master Teacher, "Jesus." The parables of Jesus are among the best known stories in the world. Though they are stories about everyday things, they pierce to the very heart of spiritual truths. As teachers, we need to use stories from everyday life to help students see the radical effects Christian faith should have in our lives. Prove that you want to learn by doing what Jesus did as a boy (Luke 2:46), asking and answering questions, one of the most ancient educational methods in the world, played an important role in the religious instruction of first-century Jewish boys.

In the Temple scene, Jesus was not "grilling" His teachers, but was asking for information. Question-asking should not be the exclusive prerogative of teachers; it is important for learning to raise questions too. In John 7:16-17, Jesus acknowledged a principle deeply imbedded in the Old Testament concept of education. God is the teacher of His people. Just as Moses received the Law from God, so Jesus identified God as the author of His teaching. Note too that one can appropriate his teachings only by doing God's will.

Learning is putting newly acquired knowledge into action. A Christian is one who not only obeys the Lord, but also learns from the teacher. The Holy Spirit is the teacher in the lives of Christians. Under His guidance, (He will lead you to the right teacher; that is full with the spirit of God.), the words of biblical revelation become a living word for each of us. As we study the recorded teachings of Jesus, the spirit gives insight into their meanings. The spirit is present at the Christian's study deck and every Christian study group, leading believers into all truth. Teaching is so important – teaching is an indispensable function and continuous process within the community of faith. Teaching is as close to the heartbeat of a congregation are fellowship, ministry and prayer (Acts 2:42). The best evangelists are those who have been educated (taught). Teaching is not just preparation for evangelism. It is a mainline evangelistic strategy. Beginning with the ministry of Jesus and continued by first century Christians, educational evangelism has always been in the forefront of the church's efforts to reach a lost world.

Evangelism is good for the purpose of going out into the world to make people better. What upset the authorities in Acts 5:25-28, was that these Christians were teaching the people in the temple area. This episode attests to the power of "instructional evangelism" as a tool for communicating the gospel. In an ideal teaching situation, an enthusiastic and knowledgeable teacher sits in intimate conversation with a highly motivated learner explaining the meaning of the word of God. Although evangelists and others are teaching-teaching is a major pastoral function (Ephesians

4:11-16). I see Paul as second to Jesus as a teacher. Because he was a skilled teacher, Paul met the Athenian intellectuals on common grounds, having demonstrated his knowledge of their poetry, philosophy and religious lore. From there he led them to the heart of the Christian gospel, some accepted the gospel and became Christians (Acts 17:22-31). Paul was a teacher from the heart. In one of the longest sojourns of his missionary career, Paul remained in Corinth for a year and a half. During that time, teaching was his primary strategy for winning the Corinthians to Jesus Christ (Acts 18:11).

The Apollos episode tells us a great deal about Christian teaching in the early church. His previous instruction "in the way of the Lord" reflected the universal practice during the New Testament period of schooling every convert in the teaching of Jesus. The spontaneous lesson in the home of Priscilla and Aquila showed that the teaching function was not restricted to "official" teachers in the church. He taught with enthusiasm and fervor, convinced of the truth. Apollos learned an important lesson. Even the skilled teacher may be corrected and taught by people with less training and skill (Acts 18:24-26). The greatest teachers do not have perfect success. Teaching the truth often leads to rejection, opposition and hardships. Teaching success is marked by faithfulness to the task, not by public popularity. Paul ended his missionary career just as he had carried it out in previous years, as a teacher. Even under house arrest in Rome, he taught Christ freely to all who came to him. Christ's rule and Lordship remained at the center of Paul proclamation and teaching (Acts 28:31). At the end of his life, Paul was still trying to make people better. Those who were schooled in the law were potential teachers of the blind, the wayward and the young. Their failure to be obedient to the law nullified that potential (Romans 2:19-24).

Likewise, we cannot teach effectively what we do not practice. Belief includes action as well as factual knowledge. A thief or adulterer makes a poor instructor in morals. A teacher should provide light for those in moral and intellectual darkness. This is possible when the intellectually superior teacher lives in moral darkness. The key to living a transformed life is cultivating a renewed mind. The persons who are too lazy mentally to drink deeply from God's revealed word or to think courageously about the meaning of personal faith will tend to be shaped by institutionalized values and socially acceptable modes of thought The teacher may become the lazy person's god. The teacher must remain and instrument through whom God can work to challenge learners to think, question and change. These persons must find God's will personally and individually. No teacher can finds God's will for me. Spiritual transformation through learning is a continuing process, not a once-for-all accomplishment. We should be able to teach one another. This practice requires that we be authentic persons whose lives are marked by genuine goodness to teach it intellectually.

The preparation for Christian teachers should focus on who they are, not just on techniques of instruction. One kind of preaching, teaching, and learning emphasizes elegant language and scintillation ideas but is devoid of spiritual energy. It can be entertaining or boringly dull. In either case, it fails to transform lives. Authentic Christian teaching does not bypass the intellect. It is predicated upon the assumption that a rational understanding of the faith must be infused with the spiritual power that reaches to the root of personality and causes the word to become flesh (I Corinthians 1:18-31).

Paul neither confessed to foolishness nor advocated it. He certainly was not arguing for an uneducated ministry. Nor was he denouncing education in general. Human knowledge is not opposed to the wisdom of God. It simply falls short of the spiritual understanding that comes through Jesus Christ. Christian teaching and learning are illuminated by the spirit, but they do not circumvent the mind. The substance of the Christian faith is intelligible and the communication of the Christian faith must be rational. The study deck and prayer closet are both essential to Christian teaching and learning. Teaching is an attempt to communicate not to display personal spiritual powers or gifts. Teachers serve learners' needs rather than satisfy personal ego problems.

The gospel tradition has been passed to Paul from faithful believers. Through careful instruction, he communicated that message to his children in the faith. Each generation of Christians must raise up faithful teachers who will pass the torch to the next generation of believers. The church depends on dedicated teachers for its continued existence (I Corinthians 15:3). Teachers are very important to the life of the believer and the church. The church must have people with the gift and calling of teaching. Those who became the professional teachers of the church deserve financial support (Galatians 6:6), teachers and learners in the church should engage in mutual support of one another, sharing personal and spiritual resources and bearing one another's loads.

In Ephesians 4:11-16, we see a special gift from God-pastors-teachers. The pastor and teacher in Ephesians 4:11, refers to the same person. Pastors are often called "preachers", but rarely "teachers." The educational function of the pastor remains an indispensable part of Christ's design for His church. Teachers build up the life and thought of the church by interpreting the revelation in Jesus Christ and applying it to daily life. They are to teach all things whatsoever Christ commanded. They give instruction in doctrine and required moral standards for believers.

Here is a learn for parents. Responsibility for nurturing children in the faith is fixed squarely on the shoulders of children's father. Obviously mothers will have much to do with the nurture and training of children (Proverbs 1:8-9), but fathers who relinquish this duty entirely to their wives do so in clear violation of New Testament teaching. "Training" is the Greek word paideia, which denotes a combination of instructions, discipline and personal guidance. Fathers are also warned about engendering anger and frustration in their children, since this will negate much of their positive teaching (Ephesians 6:4). In order to learn, there must be participation-modern educations speak of learner's active participation in the educational process. Paul advocated here (Philippians 4:8), to think, which means, to calculate, to reckon carefully. To think then is to weigh seriously the cost of incorporating the virtues listed in verse 8, into one's daily life. Paul in Colossians 2:6-8, speaks about correction. In the absence of sound teaching, distortions of truth will always rush in to fill the vacuum. Paul expressed the hope that his teaching of the believers at Philippi would establish them in the faith firmly enough to enable them to distinguish between Christian doctrine and human philosophies parading as religious teachings. Every person is a teacher as spoken of in Colossians 3:16, and every person a learner. Each of us has something to share out of our personal experiences with God. Each of us has something to learn from each other. This will happen only where the word of Christ dwells within the hearts of the people. As we sing hymns of worship and praise with grateful hearts, we teach one another. We talked about teachers and their teaching, but look out or be aware of false teachers. Ephesus was a hotbed of pagan religions, Jewish traditions and bizarre philosophical teachings (I Timothy 1:3-7). Some persons were trying to combine these into a strange conglomeration of doctrines. The church's greatest danger comes not from those who oppose Christianity, but those who want to modify Christian beliefs to suit cultural values, political doctrines and popular superstitions.

Another challenge to the integrity of the Church is the presence of numbers of unqualified persons who pose as teachers. They promote conflict and controversy rather than love, which is the goal of Christian teaching. False teachers-demonic teachings threaten the church when its teachers are deceptive hypocrites and liars (I Timothy 4:1-2). Such teachers try to set laws and legal systems in place of truth and love.

Timothy's early training under the guidance of a godly mother and grandmother was a precious heritage. This training made him a good minister or servant (I Timothy 4:6). Some false teachers are not avowed enemies of truth. They stray from the gospel because they are infatuated with novelty, like Rose Athenians who spent their time doing nothing but talking about and listening to the latest ideas (Acts 17:21). Personal pride and conceit stand behind such infatuation. This conduct leads to controversies, suspicious and quarrels rather than to peace and cooperation (I Timothy 6:3-6). Christian teaching is more than wrangling over trivialities disguised as religious thoughts. Get better so you can help make someone else better, use your gift as Paul in I Timothy 1:11, who saw both preaching and teaching as essential to his calling as an apostle and missionary for Jesus Christ. Paul also talked about the pastor-teacher having a two pronged responsibility: (1) to teach correct doctrine; and (2) to teach it in love. Only the Holy Spirit living in the pastor-teacher can ensure that sound doctrine tradition is maintained and passed on. The pastor-teacher is responsible to learn sound teaching and teach it to reliable members who will teach others. The pastor cannot monopolize the teaching function. God gives the gift of teaching to whom He will. Any church member who has the gift of teaching is responsible under God to learn from other teachers, but also study God's word personally. Such personal study should let God's word critique teachings learn from others. The word of God can be abused as well as used. It is always in danger of being distorted by teachers who handle it. Everyone is not for real or true in what they are doing. The only effective way to prevent distortion of the word of truth is diligent preparation at the study desk. Where teachers and learners are lax in their study of the scriptures, Bible classes are often filled with godless chatter and with vain babblings. Instead of becoming mature in the faith, members and teachers become ungodly. Yet they claim success because their teaching becomes so popular, spreading like gangrene, know your teachers or who is teaching you. Paul reminded Timothy (II Timothy 3:10), that his teachings and his way of life were cut from the same cloth. In fact, the way he lived attested to the authenticity of what he taught. The Bible is he textbook of the Christian faith. The scriptures are the source of religious instruction of both children and adults, pointing the way to salvation, clarifying understandings of the gospel and providing guidance for living in daily life. All doctrine must be formed on the basis of the Bible text. Teachers that are not true teachers are not always doctrinal deviationist. They sometimes prostitute truth for their need to be popular and say what people want to hear by selling their consciences in exchange for compliments. Paul warned that the task of teaching could fall into unworthy hands (II Timothy 4:3). This was because people would prefer teachers who fit their views and who taught only what their audience wanted to hear.

Self-appointed teachers-the ones that God did not give the gift to or the ones that strayed from God would arise and who would deceive others with shallow teaching, or who expounded the doctrines of men as if they were the teachings of God (Colossians 2:22). Others motivated by greed, might simply want to exploit their listeners (II Peter 2:1-3). In his role as teacher, the bishop or pastor is to communicate sound doctrine, on one hand, and refute those who oppose it, on the other. Sound doctrine is not one individual's private interpretation. It is the body of truth taught by Jesus Christ, passed on by the Apostles. Integrity is a quality found in teachers whose motives are pure. Some teach out of a need for status or self-gratification. The Christian teacher should be motivated by love for people and love for truth. Teachers must not give reason for criticism of their teaching or of their conduct. Teachers must be of a sound mind; to have their total life under control of the mind. They must show themselves to be something, teaching out of a pure motive, without desire of gain or respect of persons and purity of doctrine.

Beware of false teachers, I said it before and I say it again. One of the crucially important functions of the teaching ministry of the church is to enable Christians to recognize destructive heresies when they see them. Such heresies are based on fabricated stories rather than on scripture. This false teaching attracts great crowds, destroys the public reputation of the church and leads its followers to destruction rather than salvation. The motivation for such teaching is personal ambition and greed. The truth is not always easy to understand. Mature teachers are needed. Too many untrained and unable persons readily accept teaching positions and lead conscientious followers of Christ astray, brining destruction on both the teacher and follower. There are still teachers in the world "like" or "as" Jezebel (Revelation 2:20). The woman called Jezebel stands as a reminder of the insidious influence of false teachers tolerated by the members of a church. Through her seductive teaching, she had somehow convinced Christians at Thyatira that idolatry and fornication were acceptable.

# CHAPTER VI

# DISCIPLINE YOUR MIND

To organize your mind is to control it. The highest possible stage in world culture is when we recognize that we ought to control our thoughts. Discipline our mind with education. God is the starting point for the education that leads to wisdom.

Instruction (Proverbs 4:1-10) refers to a process of training, in which the learner submits to the teaching and guidance of a wiser person. The teaching of the mind is to have the same attitude as that of Jesus Christ (Philippians 2:5). Language reflects your character. God uses human processes and relationships to intervene in history and discipline sinful people. He can deliver a prophetic message through an enemy. He can lead a sinner to reject good advice. God works to punish human pride and rebellion. (II Chronicles 25:19-20)

Job was willing to learn from the criticisms of others. This is the mark of a wise man. (Job 6:24) Only a fool assumes that his critics are always in the wrong. Discipline your mind to be teachable. The biblical writer repeatedly emphasizes the relationship between learning and the quality of teachableness. Just as children can learn from parental discipline, so can we learn from constructive criticism all through life, if we have the humility to accept corrective advice. (Proverbs 15:31-33)

Observant parents and teachers know by experience that learners react differently to various forms of criticism and correction. Some children seem unaffected by event the harshest punishment; others whither under the mildest scolding. To a sensitive, intelligent child a rebuke can sometimes accomplish more than a hundred stripes. The wise and effective teacher stays attuned to such individual differences (Proverbs 17:10). A child's good character must be built early in life to have a good future in life. Parents can spare their children grief later in life if they will correct and guide them in their younger years. Parental discipline should always be corrective in nature, never vindictive (Proverbs 19:18).

The learner's self-discipline is more important than externally imposed discipline. The presence of good teaching does not guarantee learning, for learning is an active process in which learners seek truth and apply themselves to the task. (Proverbs 22:17) Indifference, self-sufficiency or dullness of mind and heart can close our ears to words of wisdom. We do not acquire knowledge by setting passively and waiting for it. We must search for it as though it were a hidden treasure. Human beings learn by imitating the behavior of other people. The examples others set are not always positive. Negative emotions are contagious. Children whose parents are temperamental have not choice in the matter. Brought up under the daily influence of angry parents, they learn to be hot tempered persons themselves. By self-discipline and associating with the right people, we can unlearn bad habits. We must take responsibility for ourselves and set good examples for our family, friends and associates.

## Discipline Ourselves, Don't Let Sin Reign in Your Mortal Body
### (Romans 6:12)

If you can discipline yourself to organize your mind, you will organize and manage your life to a better life, and you will surely see success and happiness. Remember, you live the way you think. The way we react mentally to anything that happens to us, that we see, hear, touch or experience, and the way we go about solving the problems it poses is what occupies our minds all the time. Remember, the way you think is the way you live. Think properly, clearly and effectively; think on things that are above and success and happiness must come to you. It is the mind that maketh good or ill, that maketh wretched or happy, rich or poor, yet we spend more time on inconsequential things than we do on organizing our minds. We should try to learn to use all of our knowledge and mental resources, at least, make an attempt to organize and discipline those resources. Just make up your mind that there is much more room for improvement, and you will make some improvements.

We must be good to please God, others and ourselves. The opposite of sin is not religion, but humble obedience. Religious rites combining what God asks and what people practice in other religions is not acceptable. To delight in false worship ceremonies rather than answer God's call to obedient service is sin. When we choose to displease God, He chooses the proper discipline for us. Sin is creative, devising evil which never entered God's mind. The ways we find to divert worship from the creator to the created seem limited, and such creative sin stretches God's patience to the breaking point. When we do not accept and learn from His discipline, He finally intervenes in a horribly creative way to destroy (Jeremiah 32:29-35) confessing sin and we recognize the justice of God's disciplinary intervention in our lives. God's word of discipline often does not sit well with the audience. A sinful people does not relish hearing God's word. Preaching does not win popularity contests. Judgment preaching (from the unpopular preacher) is in order when sin or crookedness, hostility or grudge-bearing animosity, corruption or destructiveness, and sins missing God's target dominate the life of God's people (Hosea 9:7-9).

The Church disciplines members in love to bring them to repentance. When a disciplined member repents, the Church must accept and forgive (II Corinthians 2:5-11). Each church has the responsibility to develop ways to rebuke, warn and exhort members who continue in sin. In this way, the church family encourages each other in Christian faithfulness and maturity. The Apostle Paul was disciplined by the teaching of Gamaliel's feet, which means "under his care." He was taught according to the perfect manner of the Law of the Fathers, and was zealous toward God. Remember this – a favorite student always sits directly in front of the teacher. (Acts 22:3) Be sincere about how you think or your behavior. Paul states, "I keep under my body, and bring it into subjection." (I Corinthian 9:27) Paul is saying, "When I have preached to others, will I despise myself?" In other words, the preacher must live up to his teaching. People are judged by their works and not by their words. A good person is admired by their faithfulness, hospitality and kindness. It is the life of a person that touches the heart of the people, and not his words. Sincere words come from a pure heart.

Jesus, from the day He began to preach until His death, practiced His own teaching. He taught love, and He loved even His enemies. He taught forgiveness, and He forgave those who crucified Him. He suffered many hardships and privations to move the power of His gospel. Paul states, "Mortify your members which are upon the earth." (Colossians 3:5) The body is controlled and directed by the spirit. "Mortify" in this case means "subdue." Evil desires are subdued or suppressed by means of prayer and fasting. Discipline your mind with "sound doctrine." (II Timothy 1:1-4) Sound doctrine is to promote the spiritual good of men. The mind is to become sober, earnest and vigilant. Paul in Titus 2:4-5, teaches that the young women are to be sober, to love their husbands, to love their children, to be discreet chase keepers at home, good and obedient to their own husbands that the word of God be not blasphemed. Paul is exhorting on the behavior or conduct of the woman. Also in Titus 2:9-10, Paul speaks of the man that he should have a blameless character, soundness in the faith and the ability to maintain and defend it. Those who love and practice what is good are constantly growing better, and those who love and practice evil are constantly growing worse. Every person should strive for conduct so that no one can justly say any evil of him. Speak evil of no man; falsely or unnecessarily. Kind, watchful and efficient discipline should forever be maintained in a person's life.

Efforts, not by pain or penalties, but by sound argument and kind persuasions should first be made to reclaim offenders. James states; "My brethren, count it all joy when ye fall into divers temptations"; which are trials suited to develop their character and if rightly borne, to make them better. (James 1:2)

So, bear your trials with a right spirit. To be better, you must control your tongue; watch what you say and how you say it. It is wrong to judge a person by his or her outward appearance. Have an attitude that causes you to be led of the spirit; by following His guidance. Don't walk after the flesh, which produces the works of the flesh; those to which corrupt human nature prompts, and when not restrained, produces. So, don't walk in the flesh (Galatians 5:19-21). If we live in the spirit, and if our inner life be in the spirit; that is, received from the spirit, sustained by Him, and conformed to Him in character, then let us also walk in the spirit and let our outward life also be in the spirit. In other words, let it be conformed to Him in character, so that our inward principles and outward conduct shall be in harmony with each other.

Don't be fleshly in your character. Don't mind the things of the flesh. Don't devote your time to fleshly objects. Our outward contact flows from our inward character. The flesh is to be taken as in Galatians 5:19-21, and often elsewhere, in a wide sense. It includes all earthly and corrupt passions, appetites and desires which rule in the natural heart. Be spiritual minded, it is a life manifesting itself in love, joy, peace, long suffering, gentleness, goodness, faith, meekness, temperance and all those dispositions and habits which promotes the glory of God and the good of men.

Discipline yourselves by mortifying the deeds of your body; resist, overcome and cease to gratify sinful inclinations. You must be transformed, changed in your outward conduct, and in the spirit and temper of your mind. In doing good, persons should have that wisdom and skill which results from practice, experience and habit. Don't be carnal, walking as men, selfish and worldly in your feelings and conduct. (I Corinthians 6:12) Be a good person. When you try to be good, the enemy is going to try his best to stop you. The question is, what will I do? My response will be to put on the whole armor of God, be strong in the Lord (Ephesians 6:10), as those who are united by faith to the Lord Jesus, and depend on Him for strength and all needed aid to perform every duty, bear every trial and conquer every foe. Let your conduct and intercourse of life become as the gospel of Jesus Christ (Philippians 1:27). Discipline yourself by exhibiting in principle and practice the gospel of Jesus and trust in God's grace. Then you can do it. While the gospel inoculates universal humility and benevolence, it produces these virtues in all who savingly embrace it; and thus shows itself to be divine.

Humility and benevolence are peculiarly pleasing to God. The most wondrous exhibition of them was made by Jesus Christ, and those who imitate His will, with Him receive a glorious reward, while the homage which they and all holy creatures will render Him, will show that He is God. In order to be saved, (delivered from bad intentions) men must work out their own salvation by faith, love and obedience, as God has appointed; and the fact that whenever they are inclined to do it, he works in them, and thus influences them to work out their salvation, gives them the greatest encouragement without delay to engage in this work. All men naturally love themselves with all their heart, soul, strength and mind; but, they do not love God. The gospel when embraced dethrones this idol, and leads men supremely to love God, and benevolently to seek the good of their fellow-men. Therefore, man's spirit must be trained. Man's spirit can be educated and improved just as his mind can be educated and improved. The mind can be trained and built up just as the body can be built up. This is done through the study of God's word.

To get better we must start by developing our intellect process. The process of training the mind, of building it up is a daily task. The soul of man is the part of man which deals with the mental realm; his reasoning and intellectual power. Renew, restore and save your mind or soul by the engrafted word of God (James 1:21). We must develop our spiritual life by meditating on the word of God. If you don't have anyone to teach you, then hire someone to teach you. After hearing the word, practice the word. What you have heard and received in your heart and mind, put it in action. James said that a doer of the word is one who practices the word, and when you do that, you are developing your spiritual life. When we develop our inner man, we can then dominate our outward man. Fight to win; fight to be the best that you can be. You can become that if you develop your mental and spiritual life by strengthening them. Don't be weak thinking in your mind. Don't hold on to things that will hurt you; let it go! Don't get carried away with your emotions. Don't wait for someone to help you; help yourself. You can do whatever you want to do if you just put your mind to it. All things are possible to them that believe; God will help you.

Firmly establish yourself like a tree deeply rooted, or a house on a rock. Don't let anyone rob you of spiritual blessings by leading you to depend on something besides Jesus Christ for salvation or deliverance. Trust in the love of God; for God so loved the world that He gave His only begotten Son (Jesus). Love to God and to men depend on Jesus Christ, and a desire to obey His will are the source and security of right actions; and are in all conditions and relations essential to the perfection of human character and conduct. Continue in what you believe; be not dull or slothful in it, and don't allow yourself to be in anything that can hinder it. Walk in wisdom; conduct yourself with discretion and propriety. Walk not in the counsel of the ungodly (Psalm 1); this does not embrace their principles, adopt their maxims or encourage their practices. Have a mind not to walk the way ungodly people walk. How can we do that? Meditation and prayer should be united, and the early part of each day should be spent in communion with God, and in supplication for His presence and blessings in all its duties and enjoyments. Bad company corrupts good character. Those who keep on their old life-style of doing wrong (sinning) have no saving knowledge of God. Familiar intercourse with wicked persons is corrupting.

### Better Your Communication Skills

Practice to guard your speech. You should watch what you say (Proverbs 21:2). He who guards his mouth and his tongue, guards his soul from trouble. Guarding your speech means you will be on alert for verbal patterns and habits which could cause your problems. Before you speak, you should be sure that you can live with what you say, after it is said. Choose words that will help, not hurt you and your listener. Make what you are going to say pass a mental inspection before you say it. You need to watch the way you speak, your manner and your attitude of presentation. Meditate about what you are going to say and think about who will hear it, what your tone will imply and what you want to accomplish with your words. Think about what you are going to say rather than to blurt out whatever happens to be on your mind. You need to watch when you speak and guard your timing. You need to watch for curses and learn timing in your speech, saying the right thing at the right time in the right way is cultivated art. You'll have to practice it to perfect it. One of my friends said, "My mother says, if you can't say anything good about a person, don't say anything at all."

The Bible states, "Let no corrupt communication proceed out of your mouth, but that which is good to the use of edifying, that it may minister grace unto the hearers." (Ephesians 4:29) Words that do not strengthen a person should never be spoken. Let your speech be always with grace, seasoned with salt, that you may know how you ought to answer every man. (Colossians 4:6) Seasoned language is mature, thoughtful and helpful. Here it indicates speech which gives a flavor to the discourse and recommends it to the pallet, as well as speech which preserves from corruption and renders wholesome. The conversation must not be opportune in regards to time; it must also be appropriate as regards to the person. What you say must benefit the hearers. Speak what is seasonable, pertinent, instructive and useful. Know how to answer in order to give just views and make right impressions.

## Better Communication Makes Things Better

Our behaviors are so often automatic or unconscious that we don't recognize the way we come across. We tend to take personal pride in how we as individuals have been doing or saying things all along. We resist changes in behavior and usually find it more comfortable going on as usual, getting others to change the way they do things. Study to develop more understanding. Look at the world through the eyes of other people, walking the proverbial mile in another's moccasins. Don't get caught up in phony speech. You will hurt both yourself and others if you indulge in it. You will ruin relationships and get trapped in a verbal web of deceit. Teach yourself how to speak in a straightforward manner. A person who knows how to use words wisely and well is listened to and usually accomplishes what he wants to accomplish. But, it is destructive to say something you have no right to say. Don't speak until you have thought about what you will say. Improve on the quality of your words. Don't speak until you have thought about the effect of what you will say. Pick and choose your words rather than blurting them out; and understand rather than over-explaining. Control your mouth; don't gossip. What you say must be of some value, have richness and some redeeming quality. What you say must build-up, not destroy. Your words should be a positive, elevating force. What you say must need to be said, when you say it. It must be needful for the moment. Needful words make positive contribution. What you say must give grace to those who hear. It should contribute to their happiness, be worth repeating and be said with the proper tone. Your speech is a reflection of your character and reveals you as you really are. Our use of language should be productive, helping us to reach our goals in life. Speak the truth in love. There is a right way and a wrong way to state the truth. We should be motivated by love and not embellish the facts.

Don't lie to anyone, especially to the one you love. Put some wisdom in your speech. The way of intellectual stimulation and growth is to seek to develop your wisdom and knowledge; that is you must be willing to be open to the examination of yourself and others. Nothing should escape our mouth that is not praise to God in some way. Speech belies true character. Wise action and pure living are necessary to gain a hearing from the lost. But we have to be humble minded and be willing to learn and be teachable. Being humble and having the willingness to learn is the chief characteristics of that childlike mind which Jesus Christ commends to His disciples (Matthew 11:25; Luke 2:46).

Check your attitude before you speak. Attitude is usually an important part of meaning. Many times intention and attitude are more important than plain sense. Put some hard work on changing your unsatisfactory speaking habits. Do this by examining your present speech patterns, and exchanging bad speech habits for acceptable ones.

## Eliminating Unnecessary Speech

Practice talking less and listening more. Don't respond out of emotion. Your goal is to make the situation better. Control your emotions for the sake of getting things resolved. Control your emotions that you don't cause a conflict; because conflicts are power struggles which are no-win situations. The more you argue, the more frustrated you will both become. Remember, you are not trying to get worse; you are trying to get better. Speak with the right use of words which others can understand. Don't speak to condemn. Speak things which are fitting, not finding fault with someone. Don't speak evil of no one; falsely or unnecessary. Show all meekness toward them; because true religion makes good subjects, quiet citizens, peaceful neighbors and renders others meek, patient and forgiving in all the relations of life. True religion leads those who are under its influence to be kind and courteous; and desire for others the blessings of God. The manifestation of real goodness in the habitual practice of good works, gives great joy to all benevolent beholders.

If you do good, good will come back to you. Place yourself as being a wise person; he does not need adversity to motivate him to improve. A little instruction suffices. Thereafter, he will on his own add to the knowledge he already possesses. Remain in control of yourself even when you feel anger. Never glory in your wisdom, or your strength, or your riches. Don't let riches entice you. You should have had enough sense on your own to reduce the futility of toiling for riches. Stop misusing your power of understanding to amass wealth; for you will desist from your understanding – the outcome of toiling for wealth is that one loses one's knowledge (of teaching or law of knowledge). Occupy yourself with the fear of God all day long. You need someone to teach you. If you are unable to find someone to teach you the Law of God for free, you should purchase truth by hiring a teacher. The one who helped you bear and give birth to the wisdom inside your heart.

A wise person studies a little every day until in time, he has mastered the entire Law of God. Remember, it is important to start right. A half-hearted, poorly considered effort will inevitably be a failure. You want to be the best that you can be, "Don't you?" As we try to develop our physical growth, also let us develop our social, mental, moral and our spiritual growth.

(1) Social Development – will cause you to be proud of what or who you have become.

(2) Intellectual Development – your character may be developed. Understanding, and association must come to aid it (memory becomes systematic). No longer does the mind eagerly, devour everything. You are growing now.

(3) Moral Development – your feelings should be carefully cultivated, as feeling is the root of doing. Remember, good habits are as easy to form and hard to brake as bad ones. Therefore, special attention should be given to them.

(4) Spiritual Development – your faith is confirmed. You believe in yourself. By patient, loving treatment and faithful study of God's word, doubt disappears and faith is firmly founded on a reasonable basis.

Now if you really want to be a better father, husband or wife, child, worker or even a better friend, you quicken your spiritual life by reading the Bible:

(1) Diligently (John 5:39)
(2) Prayerfully (Psalm 119:18)
(3) Thoughtfully (Psalm 119-97-100)
(4) Believingly (Psalm 119:18)
(5) Obediently (John 7:17)

A good life is worth a bushel of learning to communicate better and to understand people. Apostle Paul states, "Though I speak with the tongues of men and of angels, and have not charity, I am become as sounding brass." (I Corinthians 13:1) Our concerns should be to communicate and care for others. We reflect the company we keep. We must walk with God daily, have quiet talks with Him and make the study of His word our daily spiritual food. If we are planning to be better, then we must study the principles of being better, so if we are going to build our character, we should know the principles that make character.

Three basic principles must be kept in mind:

(1) Knowledge advances through four logical stages. All knowledge reaches the soul (mind) by way of the five senses; sight, hearing, taste, touch and smell. Through these we have sensations, and from sensations the four steps to knowledge are taken.
    (a) Perception – some cause in the outer world stimulates one of the senses; this produces a sensation. When this sensation reaches the brain, it is interpreted and we call it a perception.

(b) Conception- from a number of perceptions, take one or more common features, put them together and call the combination a conception.

(c) Judgment – by comparing several conceptions or perceptions, a judgment is formed.

(d) Reasoning – the comparing of judgments produces reasoning.

(2) Knowledge is acquired only through self-activity. Someone may instruct you, but you must put forth the effort to get it done.

(3) Knowledge must be understood and used, or it will be lost. The new truth (knowledge) must become a part of our mental development. It should make us mentally and physically strong. Knowledge is not your own until you apply it to your daily life. We know by doing. (John 7:17; Matthew 7:24) Truth so studied cleaves to the memory, quickens the intellect, fires the heart, shapes the character and transforms the life.

# CHAPTER VII

# THE WISDOM OF GOD

It has been said that a trained mind (memory) is one of the most important factors in mental organization. The person with a well-trained and organized mind is the happy and successful person. You can be a better and happier person than you are. You can put more out of that brain of yours. If you can manage to discipline (organize) your mind, you will organize and manage your life. To organize your mind is to control it. Control your thoughts so you will say the right things, or control your feelings. When you organize your thinking, you really control your thoughts and actions properly. The way we react mentally to anything that happen to us, that we see, hear, touch or experience, and the way we go about handling the problems it poses, is what occupies our minds all the time. The way you think is the way you live. Organizing your mind means you are heading toward a definite goal. If your thinking leads to action, then they are productive.

To become successful, there must be hard work applied properly and intelligently, and thinking in an organized manner. The mind is a terrible thing to waste, so don't waste it. If no one else, prove to yourself that you can be better. Now don't fool yourself and think that you are something when you are not. Before you try anything, put it in your mind first, and then try it. Work hard for what you want. Stop being afraid of failure that you set your sights on a goal you know you can easily reach. Set the level higher. Make up your mind to be a winner, work toward winning with enthusiasm. We are to think clearly and with a clear understanding. Thinking is hard. God gave us the ability to think. The reason that you can't think clearly about certain problems is that you do not have enough relevant knowledge or experience pertaining to them. If you have no knowledge of a subject, you have no starting point for thoughts; or you will think from a wrong premise and think incorrectly.

Try to think with your mind and not your emotions; which are anger, frustration, pleasure and fear. Our emotions cause us to be suggestible. We may not be able to get rid of our emotions, but we can learn to master them or hold them in check. Get rid of our bad thinking habits. Think with a sober mind. When you think, you are actually talking to yourself. We picture them in our mind and we discuss them with ourselves. In order to put good things in our mind, we will have to think on good things; like things from above, things that are lovely, kind and of peace. What you practice effectively, you will become that. What's on your mind? What are you thinking about right now? Is there power in your thinking? Are you a weak thinker or a strong thinker? Do you have creative power? If so, why not strengthen it to get what you want. If you have a goal in mind, do something about it. To try to keep a success marriage, you will have to start making the right decisions.

Knowledge is power, but we have to know how to use it. Continue to let the true knowledge that is of God flow into your mind. It is this knowledge in you that changes your attitude, behavior or conduct, and causes you to be the person that everyone will respect. The will to learn is the main ingredient for learning. Once you've got the picture in your mind of the thing you want to learn, take it step by step. Be sure you understand and can accomplish one step before continuing to the next. Once you have mastered all the steps, you can practice the things you have learned as a whole. Keep your goal in mind at all times. Remember, the way you look, the way you act, and the way you talk are the three things that's going to make up your personality. The way you think is what controls your looks, actions and words. Learn to like others first; you must learn to like people in order to really make them like you. Most people will act toward you as you act toward them. To win a friend be one; do something to gain a friend. Be a friend and you will have a friend. Don't complain about people not being kind, if you are not kind yourself. If you be kind, kindness will come back to you. Just as you like to be appreciated, show others your appreciation. Most of the time we want to change everybody, our friend, husband or wife, but the way to do that is to change ourselves. Do you want to change somethings in your marriage? I think that the most essential ingredient for a good personality is having a sense of humor. Learn to laugh a little more; laugh at yourself at the frustrations that you face, and so on. Don't be too serious all the time. Try to stop thinking about the thing that is happening to you, and a bit more about what you caused to happen. Don't let things get you down; and stop thinking too much. Maybe thinking too much is what gets you into many of your troubles. Learn also to listen attentively, listen well, and you will speak well. And if you are a good listener, you will talk better. Don't be afraid to talk. By speaking you learn to speak. Don't be a know-it-all. Don't be afraid of saying, "I don't know."

People also don't like you if you enjoy ordering them around. Don't do anything to make people dislike you. We are not always right, but we want to be, don't we? If you want people to like you, then approach them with a kind attitude. Build a library in your mind so that you will be able to discuss any subject that is being discussed. But if you have to speak, and don't know much about the subject, stand-up, speak-up, and shut-up! That means, get up, make your point as emphatically as you want to, then sit down.

## Human Intellect

In the scriptures the word of God demands full use of our intellect. Personal study brings certainty. God's people are expected to use their full intellect to interpret the materials he has inspired to pass on. Pride in human intellect can lead people to become foolish. The natural order reveals God to us. Human pride leads us to worship objects we create instead of the creator. Nothing could be more foolish; the human mind does not measure up to God's standards. The human mind makes the free choice to ignore God and follow its own wisdom. In so doing, it lets fleshly lust dominate rather than the spiritual drive to know God. Such an intellect leads people astray, causing the rejection of God Himself and leading to wholly irresponsible behavior.

God gives us freedom to choose. We know what is right and we choose what is wrong. Sin dominates our life. This is human moral and intellectual depravity. The biblical revelation places a major emphasis on the proper value and use of human wisdom. The gospel is most effectively communicated as a spiritual truth, recognizing the limitations of human intellect (I Corinthians 1:17). Human wisdom is limited when it comes to understanding the ways of God. Some people praise human intellect and exalt themselves because of accomplishments. But divine wisdom is from another nature than the human intellect, and cannot be comprehended without divine aid. (I Corinthians 1:20-25).

God's people are expected to be able to consider and to evaluate what is communicated. We are responsible under God to gather evidence and decide under God's leadership what we believe and how we should act. No other person has the authority to tell us. Such serious judgment must be founded upon the primary relationship with God. Living apart from grace blinds us to the nature and will of God. Human reason can defend any life-style because sin controls reason. Sin hardens our intellectual capacities and leads us away from the life God wants us to live. Sin gives us a consuming desire to do what is wrong. By letting human intellect control our lives, we ignore grace and choose a life that may lead to depravity.

Seeing what God has done and understanding its meaning are two different things. Perception is not only intellectual, but also spiritual. We must be properly related to God to receive spiritual insight. Such insight leads us to see that the greatest knowledge is the knowledge and will to obey God. Wisdom is a gift from God. Wisdom involves literary and musical skills, and factual knowledge. Its proper use attracts the attention of others (I Kings 4:29-34). The same God who give life also gives wisdom to His people. Biology can provide many insights into the nature of the human brain. Our distinct reasoning advantage over the animals can be explained only as God's creative gift. Just as much as life itself, intellectual attainments come from His grace. A common human failing is talking about things of which we possess no knowledge, therefore distorting the understanding of others as well as parading our own ignorance. For all the great attainments of people, human ignorance of both life and death far outstrip human knowledge. Until we know the secrets of life and death, we have no basis to challenge God's justice or His control of the universe.

The heart in the Old Testament (Psalms 90:12) is understood as the seat of the mind, the intellect, the will. Life should be so lived that people become wise as God intends. Only God can teach us to plan our lives and use our time in such a manner that we reach the full measure of wisdom He plans for us. Such wisdom leads us to accept the sorrows life brings and to be grateful for signs of God's love and care. Human intellect should lead people to remember and ponder the greatest acts of God. The wisest people ponder God's love and learn from the mistakes of other people. Human wisdom finds its basis in God's revelatory true knowledge and judgment come from the study of God's word and will, not from human philosophy and reasoning. Human philosophy helps us understand life when that philosophy is built on trust in God and His revelation.

Learning has many sources. Powerful humans build up ways to rule and control. Teachers study human traditions and use human reasoning to gain knowledge. Human knowledge or wisdom used correctly can be good and helpful, but it needs to be secondary. Genuine wisdom comes from God and the study of His word. Our intellect's purpose is to build life, not facts. To build a better life for our family and ourselves and others. God's revelation is the place to begin intellectual development.

Wisdom is made available to all who will respond. God is the ultimate source of wisdom. Those who reject wisdom have no sense of moral direction. Those who accept God's wisdom will find it a firm basis for understanding His revelation, as well as all of life's knowledge. Wisdom is revealed as the basis of all great accomplishments of humanity (Proverbs 8:1-9:16). Its origin is seen in God and was His companion in creation and is the basis of His revelation. This divine wisdom is offered to all who know and admit their own ignorance.

Do whatever it takes to learn. Long before modern education learned of a "predisposition toward learning", biblical writers pointed out that a wise and knowledgeable person is receptive to further instruction (Proverbs 9:9). Learning kindles a desire for more learning. Those seeking to develop their wisdom and knowledge are willing to be open to the examination of themselves and others. God has given people minds with the expectation that we will use them to evaluate everything we hear and see. We must decide for ourselves, not simply accept another's opinion blindly regardless of the position or education of the other person. Words expose a person's ignorance quicker than silence. (Proverbs 17:28) The search for wisdom is for more profitable than the search for wealth. How hard will you work to gain knowledge; will you work as hard as you do to gain wealth, namely money? How far will you go, (how many miles) to learn or be instructed? Will you go farther than you would go for money? But what about learning, will you do the same to go and be instructed to learn more, or gain more knowledge and wisdom?

An ingredient of wisdom is the recognition of personal intellectual need combined with the ability to accept and utilize education. Wisdom leads to careful planning for the future. Don't think about just yourself, but think about your family; plan for your family. Gain knowledge for a better home, or a better position, or maybe marriage. Being educated makes things better. Just keep reading whether it's your material or someone else's. The more you know, the more your world opens to you. The world was created of knowledge. Real wisdom recognizes its own limitations and is ready to learn more. Don't let anything rob you of the chance to improve.

Human wisdom reveals human frailties and the emptiness of most of that for which people strive. Knowledge may simply reveal more problems to be solved and more awareness of human pain that we cannot relieve. (Ecclesiastes 1:12-18) Wisdom teaches you respect, when you earn people's respect you can have greater influence on them, you don't want inheritance they may leave to you. Wisdom and monetary inheritance go well together.

(Ecclesiastes 7:11) He who possess wisdom will eventually become rich, for wisdom begets wealth. (Ecclesiastes 7:12) The first step to attain wisdom is to recognize the folly of doing wrong.

King Solomon states,

> "When I set my mind to learn wisdom and to observe the affairs that go on in the world, my eyes went without sleep both day and night. And I have seen all that God does though a man cannot comprehend the deeds that take place under the sun. For man tries strenuously, but fails to comprehend. Even if a wise man should presume to understand, he cannot comprehend them. (Ecclesiastes 8:16-17)"

King Solomon is speaking about the creation of the world from the beginning of Adam, Eve and the serpent of how death came into the world because of wrong doing. Human wisdom may enable persons to amass great pride, believing themselves to be beyond God's touch. God's judgement will show the weakness of such wisdom (Ezekiel 28:1-10). Is pride a problem to you? Solving difficult problems involve honestly admitting our limitations and seeking God's help. God can confound the wisest human. For all humanity, intellectual accomplishments, the areas of ignorance still abound. Wise leaders admit the limits of their abilities and seek persons with the needed God given skills to solve problems. What are you doing about your problems? A person's intellectual abilities are a gift from God. Their development may also come as an additional divine gift, as God reveals His purpose to people.

The ability to discern or perceive God's work comes from the wisdom which He alone imparts. God's wisdom helps us perceive that His way is the best way for us to live. Wisdom leads us to read God's inspired book and live by it.

Man makes great plans, and expects to accomplish them. We forget human intellect is always limited. We will never be wise enough to understand totally the will and purposes of God. Man will always need God. Through His revelation we can determine Hi will for our individual lives and the contribution we can make to the accomplishment of His purpose. The Bible (the Word of God) demands full use of our intellect. Luke 1:1-4, provides the example for all believers who study the gospel. Luke went to the proper source-eye witnesses, servants of the Word. He used his own skills to investigate the tradition he was given. He placed all he know into sensible order. Such personal study brings certainty. God's people are expected to use their full intellect to interpret the material. He has inspired to be passed on.

Pride and human intellect can lead people to become foolish. Human pride leads us to worship objects (cars, houses, money) we create, instead of the creator. Our minds must measure up to God's standards. The human mind makes the free choice to ignore God and follow its own wisdom. In doing so, it lets fleshly lust dominate rather than the spiritual drive to know God. Such an intellect leads people astray, causing the rejection of God Himself and leading to wholly irresponsible behavior. God gives people freedom to choose, such as where you live, the person you married, your job and your education.

# Chapter VIII

# The Wisdom of God

(James 1:5)

God's wisdom differs from the modern technical knowledge people prize. True wisdom enables us to do the right thing in the fact of moral dilemmas in light of eternal values. God is the source of this wisdom, (Proverbs 1:7) "The fear of the Lord is the beginning of knowledge, but fools despise wisdom and discipline", and it is required through prayerful communion with Him.

In James 3:13-18, he speaks of two kinds of wisdom:

> "Who is wise and understanding among you? Let him show it by his good life, by deeds done in humility that comes from wisdom. But if you harbor bitter envy and selfish ambition in your hearts, do not boast about it or deny the truth. Such wisdom does not come down from heaven, but is earthly, unspiritual and of the devil. For where you have envy and

selfish ambition, there you find disorder and every evil practice. But wisdom that comes from heaven is first of all pure; then peace-loving, considerate, submissive, full of mercy and good fruit, impartial and sincere. Peacemakers who sow in peace raise a harvest of righteousness."

Every person should pursue the wisdom of God. If you lack the wisdom of God, ask Him (God) for His wisdom (James 1:5). James is indicating that God is the giver. God will give to all who ask according to His directions. Lack wisdom here refers to feeling and acting right under all circumstances, especially in trials. All who have the Bible may be made wise to salvation, and be guided outright in all their concerns. If they are not, it is because they do not outright seek wisdom from the Lord, or knowing His will and do not obey it. Only a living personal God can know what is happening. Only a God whose wisdom is unlimited can foreknow with perfect clarity what will happen in the future. So, put your trust in God because He knows your future. The fact that God can foreknow, does not mean that He causes to happen what He foreknows, that would eliminate human freedom. Then, everything would be predetermined. We would only be doing what God programmed into us like mindless robots. God wants humans to love and obey Him on their free will. God knows us so intimately that He knows what each of us would do in any given set of circumstances. Trust in God. He is well aware of what is taking place in His world. Nothing escapes His attention. He is not a distant God, far removed from

His people, unaware of their needs or their deeds. He is not isolated by time or space. He is living and knows what is happening. God is all knowing and wisdom warns us to be aware of what we say and do because God knows us and will hold us accountable. We are responsible for this life that He has given us. God has intimate knowledge of all that happens on earth, even to the thoughts and motives of our hearts. He blesses or chastises on the basis of this knowledge, exercising His sovereignty over us and the world.

Such complete wisdom and knowledge enables Him to judge us in absolute righteousness. They do not eliminate our freedom of action and decision. We are free to do as we please, but God will judge our doing. Whether they may be good or evil. God actively follows what happens in His world, and He acts upon that knowledge. God's grace helps those who need Him. God towers over humans in His infinite wisdom. We are unable to share His wisdom. We cannot answer the deep questions Job raised (Job 28:1-28) concerning God's justice in individual cases such as Job's. Only God knows such answers. He knows what He is doing in His world. Our best wisdom is to fear and reverence God. We must trust His wisdom when our search for answers fail. God's wisdom directed His mighty acts of creation, making creation very good (Psalm 139:1-18). God's knowledge or wisdom is infinite, far surpassing anyone else's. We should learn from His warning; we cannot hide from God or deceive Him.

Human wisdom is no match for His. God will accomplish His purposes both of discipline and salvation through His authority, power and wisdom (Isaiah 29:13-21). In His perfect wisdom, God knows fully all that is happening in His world and what to do about it. Nothing is hidden from God. He knows our sins and will not ignore them. People with bad intentions will keep sinning, but people with good intentions will keep trying to stop sinning. God knows the hearts of His people. We may try to hide our sins from God, but we will always fail. Nothing escapes God's attention. You cannot sin in secret. God knows what is going on in His world and in the hearts of His people. Remember God created the world and human beings. God knows all things. He knows our true attitude to Him. His knowledge of persons and their various needs, problems and attitudes is not the detached knowledge of much information gained by study, implication or some other indirect way. Rather, it is personal knowledge which God gains first-hand in His own observation of and relationship to people. God's knowledge is not disinterested knowledge, but has a redemptive purpose. He knows each of us as individuals and seeks to deal with us on the basis of that knowledge.

The knowledge of God can deliver us from many things. Salvation, which is deliverance, comes to a person when the person responds in faith to the knowledge of God in Jesus Christ. Intellectual knowledge about God can come to people through observation of and reflection on the natural created order. With only that knowledge, people do not respond in a personal relationship to God. Only by hearing the gospel and entering into a personal faith relationship with Jesus Christ do people have saving knowledge of God. Then they gain deeper understanding of the revelation available through the natural world. The wisdom of God goes beyond the highest point of human wisdom. Human philosophies would never have thought up the Christian gospel of salvation through Jesus Christ. Those persons who have been saved by the grace of God have seen that true wisdom which comes from God.

God Himself is not known by human wisdom, nor is He found at the end of an argument. God is known only when He reveals Himself and we respond to that revelation in faith. Humans cannot know everything God knows and plans. People can have the spirit to reveal Jesus Christ's mind in a specific decision. Grace is not an emotional act separated from intelligence and purpose. God is wise as He distributes His grace to us. He clearly is accomplishing a predetermined plan as He reaches out to us in His saving love. God is a purposive God whose wisdom informs and guides His every action. God's sharp word shows us where we are wrong, not only in what we do, but in how we think and feel. We would like to hide our guilt, but we cannot. God has perfect knowledge of what is going on in this world, even to the point of knowing the very thoughts of our hearts (Hebrews 4:13). God's knowledge should reassure us. He knows our expressions of love in word and deed. Our consciousness of sin should be set at ease by our realization of His love controlling our lives. Then we have no reason to fear in His presence (I John 3:19-20).

## Chapter IX

# Subject to Family Responsibilities

Human life has been given an environment conducive to growth and entrusted with the responsibility for using it well. A part of being in God's image is responsibility. That responsibility focuses upon the fact that only God can give life. It also involves humanity's responsible use of procreating powers. Beyond this, human responsibility includes the proper exercise of control over all the rest of the world and its creation.

When family has problems (conflict) it is wrong to allow them to go on without letting the teachings of God's word help bring about resolution of conflict. Jealousy between children, plus parental partiality, breeds dishonesty and deception. The consequences are a divided family, frequently producing hatred, lack of trust, and dissolution of the family itself. Deep and divisive problems within a family lead members to substitute rejection for acceptance. Acceptance is the only basis for family life. Rejection frequently simmers below the surface until grief or loss brings it into light.

Respect and love for parents often keeps the lid on such rejection and hatred of others establishes the foundation for the possibility of more violent acts. Family treachery can be overcome when the victim takes the initiative in offering forgiveness. Individuals are responsible for their own acts of wrong doing and must except the responsibility to refrain from wrong doing. Blaming other people is not an escape from responsibility for doing wrong. A person must bear full responsibility for personal acts of unfaithfulness.

The sinful act against another person is a sin against God. Such a sin demands renewing the relationship with the other person, as well as renewing the relationship with God. You are responsible for what your mouth utters in every moment of life. God's people are to love God completely and to teach that love to their children. They are to inform their children of God's history of salvation. Election by the loving God is a call to love God and live responsibly before Him.

There should be a close tie and corporate solidarity of the family. The sin or wrong doing of one person seriously affects and can have serious consequences for each member of the family. It also reveals that my sins or wrong doing seriously affect those closest to me. Our responsibility is to keep our family safe. It is also the parent's responsibility to be the models for the need of God's guidance in the nurture and education of children. Watch out for the destructive effects of deceit and quarreling of personal relationships. It exemplified tragically in the story of Delilah and Samson (Judges 16:4-22) It also demonstrates graphically how the word "love" can be used in a relationship which reveals no indication that love exist at all. Samson was apparently drawn primarily by sexual attraction, and Delilah showed no concern for his welfare when offered money to betray him.

Relationships based on feelings such as these have little chance for survival. Only faithful commitment can overcome conflicts and competing loyalties. Speaking about "love", everyone in the family needs to be loved, even the in-laws. Ruth's fervent speech to her mother in-law Naomi is one of the most beautiful declarations of authentic family love (Ruth 1:15-18). Even though not addressed to husband-wife relationships, it is often used in wedding ceremonies to describe what marital love should be. It affirms the desire to be together, to be family, and to worship the same God. All of these elements are central to a healthy marriage. The responsibility of parenthood means devoting prime time to loving and training children even if other good works must be left undone. Parental responsibilities can be neglected by parents while doing important things. To be sure that family life is not usurped so drastically by other concerns, mothers and fathers are faced with making the best choices for the use of their time when children are young.

Friendships are good parents. Family ties should give members freedom and encouragement to develop strong relationships outside the family. In I Samuel 18:1-4, in spite of his father's jealousy of David, Jonathon loved David as though he was a brother and was willing to defend David against his father's anger. This fact illustrates the depth of commitment in a true relationship and Saul's personal weakness in not feeling his son to enter the relationship openly. Family therapists indicate that families who have such friendships are generally happier in their own relationships. Children need complete training. Unwillingness to confront children when their actions are contrary to family expectations encourages them to continue those acts. David failed to exercise parental responsibility in this case (I Kings 1:6). The long-range result was revolt and death for David's son. Everyone needs to know how to live socially and spiritually. They must learn how to trust in God by studying the Bible. Parental love and teaching is the biblical model to lead children to God. No other institution can be more effective than the home. Be good to children. Children add richness and joy to life. They are blessings from God. Grandchildren bring joy and hope to aging adults. Wisdom in Proverbs 1:8-9, is intellectual, experiential and religious.

Parental guidance was the inspired writer's model for the teacher-student relationship. Parental teachings are basic to family living and to society's larger educational program. Parental teaching helps young adults avoid tragic mistakes. Strong contrasts are made in Proverbs 12:4, between wives who are acceptable in their behavior and those who are not. The good wife is valued as a gift from God, but the bad wife is generally a quarrelsome one. The good wife is respected by her husband and brings honor to his name. Only a relationship of trust and commitment from both parties can lead to the respect and honor needed for family success.

A good lesson is not to judge one another. Good communication is at the heart of good human relationships. This is especially true of family relationships. These verses, Proverbs 15:1, 4, 23, celebrate gentleness, encouragement and appropriateness in verbal communication. Proverbs 18:2, 13, 17, point out common communication faults that cause tension in personal relationships. Honesty in speech is contrasted with using humor that hurts. Open confrontation is described as better than refusal to care enough to face issues. Poor communication destroys family relationships. Communication faults which lead to interpersonal tension include the love of one's own voice rather than love of wisdom, the failure to listen, and the inability to discuss questions frankly and openly.

The maintenance of family relationships is the responsibility of each member of the family. Bad family relationships destroy its members. The family should teach cooperation through shared responsibilities and joint projects. Every person has a beginning in life, they are childhood and youth. Youth is the time of development and experimentation. The young should find satisfaction in their youth, but must recognize they are still responsible to God for all youthful acts. While not to be belittled, undue value should not be placed upon youth as such. A generation which strives for youthfulness has missed the point of life itself, for youth is only an introductory stage of life.

For a better marriage: "love" involves the whole person in an intensity of feelings for the other which expresses itself both in desire for that person and in self-giving to that person. The marriage relationship involves three types of love: (1) sexual love, (2) friendship love, and (3) self-giving love. Such love outlives death and produces a protective jealousy which allows no competition. Marital love is commitment and trust forever. It cannot be destroyed, nor can it be purchased. God gives such love to two people committed to Him and to one another. Dedication love between marriage partners should bring fulfillment and contentment. The thought or sight of the beloved should flood the lover with happiness and joy. The end result of shared love is contentment. "Don't hate", family ties are supposed to bind people together. When hatred breaks such ties, the tragedy is extreme. We face death, the punishment for sin or wrong doing, strictly because of our own sins or the wrong doing of parents, which do affect their children. We have to live in the environment that our parents create. Everyone should use their interest and skills for spiritual growth. Learning how to forgive is a great responsibility in a Christian family life. Everyone should try to be better, because so many people that you are not aware of need you. Don't let anyone help you more than you help them; it is better to give than to receive. Can you surely love someone who hates you? There are two kinds of love; lip love and action love. What you are saying and what you are doing, do they match up?

Good family relationships bring joy and times of difficulty bring grief, but grief can be turned into joy – just as the joy of having a child over comes the pain of childbirth. Joy is a gift of God. Shared family experiences of joy create memories that continue through life. Families need to guard against letting the difficulties of daily tasks rob them of time to plan enjoyable experiences together.

Within the family of the kingdom of God, Jesus' relationship with His disciples becomes one of friends loving one another. Friendship is a close intimate relationship in which affection can be expressed freely. The heart of such friendship is the willingness even to give one's life for a friend. Families can develop friendships within the established role relationship of husband and wife, and parent and children, as Jesus and His disciples became friends even though He never ceased being Lord.

Love in the family must be the real thing expressed in action, not merely in words. There must be a loving behavior and described as one of a sincere love, and respect-to honor one another is to show respect for the other's personhood. Such respect is essential to Christian home relationships as well as to life in the Church. Husbands are to treat their wives with respect; wives are to respect their husbands; children are to respect their parents; and parents are to discipline children while still showing respect and sensitivity for the child's emotional and spiritual needs. Families should pursue the grace of hospitality, a quality of caring which families can practice throughout their homes.

Make your marriage better. Sexual union is God's plan to create physical and emotional unity in the marriage relationship. Such unity is the foundation of the family. Sexual activity is a demonstration of commitment and unity within the family. Husband and wife share a mutual responsibility for the sexual fulfillment of the marriage partner. Christians cannot claim private possession of their own bodies since in the one-flesh relationship husband and wife belong to each other. Sexual needs are part of human nature created by God. The marriage relationship is the only relationship in which sexual needs can be truly satisfied. The husband and wife should pray together. Marriage is designed for permanence. Divorce must not be seem as an easy option to escape problems. Being married to one another should commit themselves to each other and working out problems in the relationship.

There are plenty of responsibilities that should be spread around; marriage, children, etc. with economic support. Parents are to provide for their children. Adult children do have personal financial responsibility for aged parents (I Timothy 5:4, 8, 16). Economic support is still a primary function of the family even though governmental support systems are often necessary and can be used legitimately. Every person in the family home has a responsible relationship role to play-husband and wife, parent and child. In each case self-giving of one to the other is described. For the wife, it is a voluntary yielding in love to her husband's headship in the home. The husband is to yield himself to his wife in the same spirit that Christ Jesus yielded Himself to the cross to establish the Church. Children are to submit themselves to their parents in obedience, and fathers are to give themselves to the task of guidance and discipline for their children (Colossians 3:18-21).

Mutual submission does not define how individual families will determine role responsibilities in the home. It affirms a new attitude of voluntary submission in love from each family member based upon Christian faith. Submission as a Christian's attitude is basic to social life in the gospel (Romans 13:1-7; Titus 3:1; and Hebrews 13:7). It refuses to use other people as objects, and it understands authority as servanthood.

Biblical faith places a high priority on the family. Meeting the physical needs of one's family is a part of Christian stewardship. Christians should manage personal resources in a responsible way to care for family needs. Relationships should honor the Lordship of Jesus Christ over the home and demonstrate to the outside world the power of the Word of God. The love shown in a Christian home should overcome non-Christians' arguments against Christianity. The important personal self-control and self-giving is that the outsiders may not be able to criticize the behavior of Christians. The responsibility of the marriage vows must not be taken lightly. Marriage means fidelity and commitment to one's spouse. The prayer of a husband and wife is important and must not be hindered by misunderstandings in the relationship. The physical strength of men should not become an obstacle to the joint humility required in any praying together.

# BIBLIOGRAPHY

Holman. <u>Disciple's Study Bible.</u> New International Version: Nashville, Tennessee: Holman Bible Publisher.

King James Version. <u>The Holy Bible</u>. Holman Bible Publisher: Nashville, Tennessee.

Jay P. Green, Sr. <u>The Classic Bible Dictionary</u>. Sovereign Grace Trust Fund: Lafayette, Indiana, 47903, 1988.

Printed in the United States
By Bookmasters